MY PROSTHETIC LIFE

A Memoir **LAURA KENDALL**

Copyright © 2022 by Laura Kendall

All rights reserved.

No portion of this book may be reproduced in any form without written permission from the publisher or author, except as permitted by U.S. copyright law.

Cover design by Ryan Mulford.

To my husband, John who loves me unconditionally, supports me vigorously, holds me up even when it's not easy, and who is the love of my life.

TABLE OF CONTENTS

Introduction
Chapter One: Who in the Hell Do You Think You Are, Laura?
Chapter Two: What Exactly Are You Afraid Of?
Chapter Three: Out of the Fog
Chapter Four: The Roles Unchosen
Chapter Five: Keeping My Friends Close
Chapter Six: Keeping My Enemies Closer
Chapter Seven: Feelings...Nothing More Than Feelings
Chapter Eight: My Happy Place
Chapter Nine: Parenting – No Judgment – It Just Is
Chapter Ten: Patterns That Built Me
Chapter Eleven: Motherhood: Not for the Squeamish
Chapter Twelve: Hands Down...The Most Pivotal Point in My Life
Chapter Thirteen: My Mechanical Journey
Chapter Fourteen: Dream On
Chapter Fifteen: The Last Hurrah
Chapter Sixteen: Learning to Run
Chapter Seventeen: Going to Hell Slowly in a Hand Basket
Chapter Eighteen: Making the Same Mistakes
Chapter Nineteen: The Last Snow Day
Chapter Twenty: Second Verse – Same as the First
Chapter Twenty-one: Music is My Life
Chapter Twenty-two: A Brush with Celebrity
Chapter Twenty-three: Make Your Own Kind of Music
Chapter Twenty-four: Styx and Stones
Chapter Twenty-five: THE END

Introduction

Most people know that we are all different. I decided to share my story because I feel I have something to say on the subject and speak to those who are challenged by a birth defect, an unfortunate accident, or any condition another person might judge while not walking in another's shoes. Sometimes it helps to know we are not alone in our frustrations and difficulties. Universally, I would like this memoir to be relatable to anyone who feels different no matter what his struggles may be. It doesn't matter that my story is about being born without a left wrist and hand. The reader could be struggling with their weight, some type of addiction, racism, or any kind of difference - visual or not. Anyone can relate to these kinds of struggles no matter where they come from.

Some unexpected surprises occurred during this project. Memories came flooding back. The good ones made me happy. I smiled a lot while writing this memoir. Difficult and painful situations afforded opportunity to heal. I kept you, the reader, in mind. I hope my words and experience are helpful, enlightening, and useful for healing in your lives as well. My wish was to gain more peace through resolve and share an understanding with anyone who has ever been in my shoes. I have always wondered what my purpose on this earth is. Maybe this is what I'm meant to do in order to help others in similar situations. No one should have to feel alone.

My story might be for you, not only if you want to get to know who I am, but to understand the struggles and successes of being born with a birth defect, and how to accept change. I hope you will take this journey with me!

"There is nothing to writing. All you do is sit down at a typewriter and bleed."

~ Ernest Hemingway

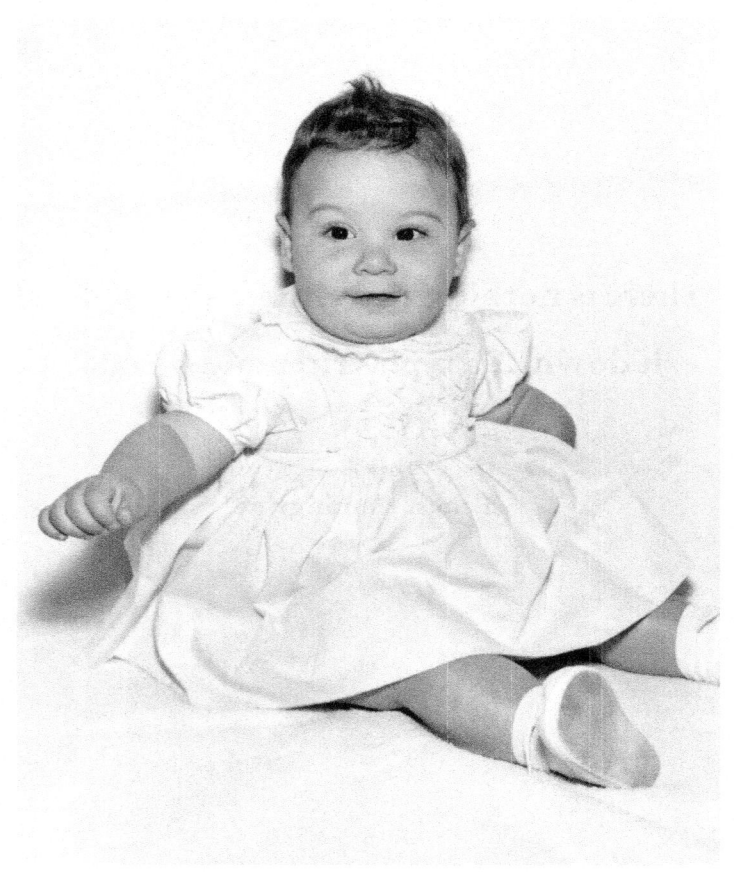

Chapter 1

Who in the hell do you think you are, Laura?

Doesn't everyone have a different idea or opinion of who we are? We are judged by family, friends, acquaintances, and strangers differently, aren't we? Even those who know us best have their own ideas of who we really are on the inside. We are critiqued by what is seen on the outside mostly. Our responses, reactions, expressions, and body language dictate how we are viewed by others; not by what we actually feel. We are the only ones who really know who we are physically, mentally, emotionally, and spiritually. Some of us have known all our lives. Some have learned, along the way, who our true selves are by keeping what is beneficial, or simply good for us, and discarding what is not. Some of us have had the opportunity to choose who we want to become to lead happy, fulfilled lives. Some of us have chosen to stunt our growth by staying in the familiar ways of living because it's comfortable and cozy.

I have felt misunderstood most of my life. I was told by a co-worker emotion is my worst enemy. I suppose this statement is true in the workplace. Perhaps this is the primary reason I never wanted to be in a supervisory position. I was never very good at playing poker either! Some may call my being misread as a lack of effective communication. Some attribute this to wearing my heart on my sleeve. In any case, I believe my emotions are indicative of my true self. I spent most of my life stuffing them down and being fearful of them. I was taught emotions were typically a negative attribute, especially for women in my family. Men are logical. Women are emotional negating any thought or opinion as being rational. Surely, a feeling based on matters of the heart is "just a woman thing". Even if that statement were true, I'll take emotions and real feelings over having none at all. I spent too many years running from them. It turns out it really doesn't matter. Everything I feel is written all over my face anyway.

What others think of me is none of my business. Not everyone is going to love me, or even like me. Do I still care a little? Of course. I am still a work in progress. With that I am beginning my story with The End. I have written my own eulogy. This is not to be morbid or dramatic. This writing assignment became very personal, quite healing and reminded me of a piece read at a memorial service many years ago. "The Dash", a poem written by Linda Ellis, has always resonated with me. I believe the space between our birth and death dates represents everything about ourselves as a whole. Even though I shouldn't care about others' perceptions, I thought it important to share who I think I am. My own eulogy is not to convince anyone to change his mind, but to understand my story better based on my history, experiences, and most importantly, how hard I have worked on being a better person today than I was yesterday.

Laura's Eulogy

Most of you don't know me, but I became Laura's closest, dearest friend after more than half her life had been lived. I watched her being born and wondered if her life would ever be less painful and difficult with her physical difference. I cried along with everyone else on her birth day and on many days that followed as I watched strangers point and stare. Would she ever be able to have a normal life, get married, have children, maybe learn a trade, or have a career?

I think this quote, written by Bernice Johnson Reagon, is exactly how Laura chose to live her life: "Life's challenges are not supposed to paralyze you, they're supposed to help you discover who you are."

Laura's challenges may have seemed obvious to others. Sure...some of her struggles were learning to do daily tasks with one hand. Those obstacles were easy for her, although some took longer to master than others. Those who knew her best also knew the biggest challenges were just like most of us: to find our own answers to why we are here.

What is our purpose and place in this world? Who are we?

These answers took years of actually living, instead of just going through the motions, just as it does for most everyone. I hope you all remember Laura as someone who she believed she became. A woman who loved deeply with everything in her being. Her husband, John, was her best friend, the love of her life and partner in all things. Her daughter, Michelle, was a part of herself and heart – the only one who knew what her heart sounded like from the inside. LauraSue, the granddaughter she never thought possible, was her ultimate joy. She was never able to describe how differently this love felt except for feeling like her heart was beating outside of her chest.

I tried to imagine what Laura would want everyone to know when I was asked to write this eulogy. She had some regrets, but none she hadn't made peace with. She lived as if each day was her last. Some days it meant having no money. Some of those days were her happiest. Some days it meant trying to fit 20 pounds in a ten-pound bag by trying to do more than what was possible in one day. Most days it meant being genuinely happy and content with life. She was always grateful for having all of you to love and teach her how to live. She knew how to have fun. Crying and laughter were her favorite emotions; especially when they happened in that order.

She believed in forgiveness. It was the only way she could let go and move on. It never meant giving someone who had hurt her a front seat in her life. It meant lessons learned, having real compassion, giving second chances – not four – and healing – the only way she could have an open heart.

If Laura were here, she would say get busy living. Right now is all you have. Love with everything you've got, share your life openly and trust your instincts. Believe in yourself. Live happy. Chase your dreams. It's why we're all here.

My disappointments and accomplishments go hand in hand. No pun intended! HA! I spent most of my life disappointed that I was born different. This included feelings of anger, sadness, depression, inadequacy, and not wishing to be **like** other people, but actually **being** them. I frequently fantasized about wiggling my nose like "Bewitched", the 60's sitcom with Elizabeth Montgomery portraying a witch. I could clap my hands, transfer items between both hands while doing the dishes, tie my shoes without having to wear a heavy, obtrusive, uncomfortable prosthesis - if only I could twitch my nose. I could also be rich, prettier, happier, smarter, and be everything I am not. Hey, it's my fantasy!

It's interesting and gratifying that most of my accomplishments have come to fruition because of my disappointments. I had to work very hard to be successful in activities taken for granted by someone with two hands. I was the only child in kindergarten who could tie shoes. So, I got to tie all the kids' shoes on the playground. I remember feeling so proud; that is until my report card came out and the comments read, "Laura always wants to be first in line". Although I had a physical "handicap", I was still an only child!

I learned to type in a vocational business college through the California State Rehabilitation Department. I enrolled in the Stenographer Program and learned to type 55 words per minute and shorthand at 70. Choosing a dead-end career with my learned skills was yet another disappointment. Who wants to be a secretary? No one chooses that do they? Don't get me wrong. I am grateful for knowing how to type. It allows me to get what's in my head in black and white much faster than using a pen. I really enjoy typing. It's one of few things I do well and makes me feel proud. I just should have used business college to get into journalism instead of clerical assistant positions and eventually accounting related jobs. I was the one crying at the dining room table trying to do math homework. My parents didn't know anything about the "new math" and couldn't help me either. My employment history shows a method of survival instead of fulfilling, gratifying career choices. But here I am now doing what I love – writing. I can be grateful for that.

All my dreams, disappointments and accomplishments were fear based. According to Merriam-webster, "fear is an unpleasant and often strong emotion caused by anticipation, or to be afraid or apprehensive." I thought my arm would be the catalyst and excuse for never feeling whole, being uncomfortable with myself forever, and unconsciously sabotaging relationships with bad choices. As it turns out, fear has been much more than that.

"Perhaps the greatest risk any of us will ever take is to be seen as we really are."

~ Cinderella

Kindergarten

Chapter 2

What exactly are you afraid of?

Fear has been a major part of my life for as long as I can remember. I felt anxiety every time I met someone new, a new school year began, any time I would have to be without my arm (like summer and swimming), and while hearing the inevitable question, "What happened to your arm?" I got so tired of bucking up and being brave. It seemed like I would never feel unafraid until a friend in recovery made a deal with me to walk through the fear together. Cheryl had scars on her arms that looked like you would see on a burn victim - except hers where from intravenous drug use. She rarely wore short sleeves because the discolored, shriveled skin looked a little scary. I imagine others probably thought of my arm in the same way with or without the prosthesis. We went to the water park, stripped our clothes down to our swimsuits, held hands and walked through our self-conscious, self-absorbed and scary journey together. That was the first of two times I felt good about being on public display. I finally had a friend who could personally relate to my own feelings after 36 years of doing it alone.

One of my biggest fears has always been not being completely happy. I was terminally uncomfortable on the inside because of what I was missing on the outside. I remember hearing "Beauty is only skin deep, but ugly is to the bone," a quote by Dorothy Parker. This popular saying was supposed to mean that a person's character is more important than how one looks. My identity has always been based on how I look and/or how I have been perceived by some. At least that's what I always thought. Therein lies my confusion. How could I be beautiful inside and out with my difference sticking out like a sore thumb? No one is perfect, but I had a head start on everyone else.

It turns out the route to my own happiness was inside myself all along. Love comes from within. "Laura, you will never be able to love anyone until you love yourself," my ex-husband Danny said. I wasted so many years being overly self-conscious about my outer shell rather than looking inside to get to know and love my own authentic, true soul. What happened next would change me forever.

"You can never cross the ocean unless you have the courage to lose sight of the shore."

~ Christopher Columbus

Me and Lorri

Chapter 3

Out of the Fog

My self-consciousness course of life changed when we went on a cruise to Alaska with some friends several years ago. We had to fly from Sacramento Metropolitan Airport to the port in Vancouver, British Columbia. Unfortunately, this required an airport security check point as well as getting on an airplane. Neither is one of my favorite things. I am absolutely terrified of flying so my little girlfriend brought me a valium to take before our flight.

My bestie, Lorri and I have been friends since we were Freshmen in high school. Our lifelong bond began when we learned our names weren't the only similarity we have in common. To this day she hates being called Laura as much as I'm not fond of being addressed as Lorri. Our birthdays are also a day apart and we still celebrate them together every year in some way – mostly dinners out with our spouses.

Lorri and her husband, Mark, had already gone through security and were at the gate. We were a bit behind them because John and I had to fix our cigarette addiction one more time before being in a non-smoking zone. We both removed our shoes, placed our loose items in the basket, sent our carryon luggage through the x-ray machine and walked through the metal detector. Dreading the inevitable, I was not surprised when the buzzer sounded, as my hook was aluminum and God only knows what made up all the internal mechanics. A very nice, male, security agent ran the handheld detector over my body. "Ma'am, please hold your arms out while I run this scanner over you". Then he explained he was going to swab my prosthesis for a bomb or remnants of any weapon ammo. He cleared me to proceed. NOT SO FAST! The next thing I saw was a HUGE woman with long dreadlocks walking toward me. She was even scarier than my thinking about getting on the airplane. She told me she was going to swab my arm. The nice gentleman told her he had already done that. She replied, "I'm going to do it AGAIN". She led me away from the line, but still within earshot and visibility of other passengers. She proceeded to run the handheld detector over me. She instructed me to turn around and said, "I'm going to run this over your back". I remember exactly how self-conscious, embarrassed, and mortified I felt in front of everyone. So – just like something I would do to ease my own tension, I asked her with a giggle, "Oh you're going to back hand me?" She said, "That's not what I said, MA'AM". I told her I was kidding with a shaky voice. She said, "I don't KID at work, MA'AM". I barely remember grabbing my carryon from the baggage conveyor belt. My heart was pounding. I was shaking all over while trying to hide my emotions. The original male agent mouthed to me "I'm so sorry" as I was leaving the area. I burst into tears - no longer able to hold anything inside. My husband saw a supervisor grab the female monster agent and take her out of the area. John missed his calling as an FBI agent because he sees EVERYTHING. He can describe everyone in a restaurant after we leave right down to the color and type of clothing. It may be a good thing I didn't see her being questioned. I might have yelled something like "SERVES YOU RIGHT BITCH!". Instead, my husband held me while I buried my head in his chest and sobbed.

Being the best husband ever, John asked me if I wanted to go shopping - in the airport. He knows just what to do! I said, "YES!"

We met back up with our friends after a little browsing in the airport shops. Lorri took one look at me and knew exactly where we were headed – the bar. I began telling them what just happened as the bartender mixed our Bloody Marys. He interjected his opinion and gave us the information of how and where to report Monster Agent. I washed down my valium with the second Bloody Mary and we boarded the plane. The next thing I remember was my husband nudging me with his elbow. I opened my eyes to the sound of the third "HONEY". My chin was still pointing downward into my chest and my tongue was completely out of my mouth. John said, "PUT YOUR TONGUE BACK IN YOUR MOUTH! I THOUGHT YOU WERE DEAD!" I looked at my girlfriend sitting an aisle over and asked her, "WHAT? You didn't get a picture of that?" She said, "I couldn't" with the sweetest smile on her face. I'd have done it to her in a minute just for the laugh later! It's probably an image she'd like to forget, though. I'm sure.

The return airport experience was completely different. The security agent told us to place our loose items in baskets before going through the metal detector as usual. I said, "Well, you're gonna love this", removed my prosthesis and put it in the basket. We all looked at each other and laughed. WHY OH WHY hadn't I ever done this before? That one second of self-consciousness was so much better than all the time spent going through security with my arm on! The point is, since that horrible story with Monster Agent, my airport insecurities are gone. It's actually pretty amusing now. I just throw my arm in the basket, walk through the detector and stand at the end of the conveyor. I get to enjoy watching the agents as they try to figure out what is going through the x-ray machine. I watch them move the image on their screen back and forth a couple times. I'm the one standing at the end of the conveyor laughing and pointing at an arm without my prosthesis. I'm amused if no one else is!

"One day you will tell your story of how you overcame what you went through and it will be someone else's survival guide."

~ Brene Brown

Left – my daughter Michelle
Right – her daughter LauraSue

Chapter 4

The Roles Unchosen

Role 1 – Only Child

I can't ever remember being glad about being an only child. Even today, in my sixties, I am still able to feel exactly as I did growing up: lonely, depressed, bored, and longing for someone to talk to but too afraid to reach out to anyone for fear of being perceived as needy.

My sister, Michele, was born around 17 months after me. She had multiple internal issues like an underdeveloped heart, cysts on her malformed kidneys and other abnormalities no one else remembers. She only lived about an hour and my parents are the only ones who were able to see her. She was very fair- skinned and had features that resembled my mother, unlike me who looked, and still looks, more like my father.

We were both born with problems. Mine was external with an underdeveloped left arm (without a wrist or hand). Michele's abnormalities were internal and unfortunately fatal. All our imperfections and issues were supposedly due to medication prescribed by my mother's doctor to treat morning sickness. It had initially been determined that Thalidomide, the most well-known drug to cause birth defects, was not the cause. Those assumptions were believed to be true by my mother. She had no reason to believe otherwise.

I discovered an article from the New York Times written by Katie Thomas, entitled <u>The Unseen Survivors Want to be Heard,</u> while researching birth defects and writing this chapter. This article was originally published March 23, 2020. The following excerpt caught my attention immediately:

> *"The man on the bus was staring at her. Carolyn Farmer, 17, noticed him as she closed the Leon Uris novel "Exodus" and gathered her things.*

It was 1979, and she knew what it was like to have strangers gawk at her. She had been born with shortened arms and fingers missing on each hand.

Are you a thalidomide baby? he asked as she waited to get off..."

Carolyn's answer was no. Unlike her, I have heard that word many times before. Particularly all the times my mother said, "It wasn't thalidomide because those babies had serious deformities instead of being underdeveloped like Laura".

The following information from Katie Thomas' article led me on an unexpected search for the truth:

> *"Thalidomide, a sedative sold by a German drugmaker, was said to relieve everything from anxiety to morning sickness, but it led to perhaps the greatest pharmaceutical scandal of all time. About 10,000 babies, many in*

Germany, Britain and Australia, were born with severe defects in the 1950's and 1960's after their mothers took it. Some babies had no arms or legs. Others had no ears or malformed kidneys.

The scandal briefly flared in the United States, where the drug was given to about 20,000 Americans in loosely run clinical trials sponsored by two American drug makers. The crisis led to passage of modern drug safety laws in the United States that required pharmaceutical companies to prove their medicines worked through rigorous clinical trials.

But the babies whose mothers took thalidomide in the United States were largely forgotten. Today, more than half a century later, people who believe they are the U.S. survivors of thalidomide have found one another through Google searches and Facebook groups, joining forces to fight for justice, recognition and compensation."

At the time of this writing, I am still in the depths of my research and discovery. I do believe, however, I am a survivor. I have become a member of several thalidomide groups and will consider writing another book devoted to this subject. For now, I am choosing to keep the integrity of my story intact.

Because there was no reason to believe my mother's daughters were both born for any other reason than genetics, my mother took her doctor's advice and agreed to a tubal ligation (fallopian tubes tied). She was led to believe she was unable to have "normal" babies. So, I became an only child – my first real role.

Role 2 – Best Friend

My best friend, Claudia, was the closest I would ever come to having a sister - my favorite role. We have been friends since the day we met in 1964 (over 50 years). We stood by each other from first through 12th grades and made it through puberty together. We compared our legs the first time we shaved and anxiously awaited our breasts. She would say she's still waiting for hers if you asked Claudia right now! We called each other's parents Mom and Dad. We were each other's maid of honor at our weddings and saw our families begin with both of our daughters. We have been there for each other in good and tough times. She has always been more than my best friend. She is my confidant, my rock and my unconditional, nonjudgmental sister.

Claudia had three older brothers as well as a sister who is about four years older than us. I have always been grateful for being a member of her family – the family I would never have. I never felt different in any way or like an outsider. We even fought like sisters – mostly when I wasn't getting my way. I was an only child after all! I can remember standing in front of my door begging Claudia to stay longer so I wouldn't have to be alone. I remember another time slamming her brush into her hand because she wanted to leave. OMG! I was such a needy brat and she loved me anyway! She still does even though her memory is far better than mine. I'm certain she is still capable of making me cringe with a story about my bad behavior as a child. I shiver just thinking about it!

We have seen each other laugh until we couldn't breathe. We could send ourselves into hysterics just recording our silly voices on an old reel to reel tape recorder. I can't count the times we were told to be quiet during sleepovers, but it only made the giggling worse.

We have also seen each other cry our hardest. We were 18 years old when her father passed away unexpectedly from a massive heart attack. Logic tells me there is no possible way I could feel as heartbroken as Claudia, but it sure felt like I had lost my dad too. It was our first real loss and we were both hysterical. Although I have had and still have more than one best friend to this day, Claudia remains my #1, oldest and dearest one. She will always represent and hold the original title of Best Friend.

Role 3 – Cry Baby

Although I have been called a cry baby, I have learned it's not a terrible role anymore. I proudly wear that label now and am grateful I can cry without feeling embarrassed or being shamed for my behavior. There were many times I have felt sorry for myself for not being like the other kids and desperately wanting to have two hands. Just a simple task like not being able to clap my hands was a reminder that I wasn't a regular kid. Snapping both fingers on both hands, doing cartwheels, playing on the "monkey bars" and playing softball – oh that was a real scream. I would try to catch a ball and take it out of the glove quickly so I could throw the ball afterwards. I HATED physical education! I know firsthand how it feels not being picked for a team. The only good thing about P.E. was not having to take a shower with the other girls (because of my arm). Looking back I wonder how I got out of the humiliation of stripping in front of everyone. It was easy enough to take my prosthesis off along with all my clothes. Maybe the teachers didn't know that. Or maybe my parents let me get away with it. I don't know, but I felt like I got at least one break. For me – taking off my arm was worse than exposing my naked body.

My dad would say, "WHY are you crying NOW?" It didn't matter if I had fallen off my bike and skinned both knees, or sobbing because I was frustrated with life. It wasn't ok. So, I spent many years locking myself up in my room so I could cry without anyone knowing. I learned turning sadness into anger was a much easier emotion to feel as well. I found out later using drugs was an escape for not feeling anything. Then one day I realized there wasn't a substance that worked anymore. I ended up at a Narcotics Anonymous meeting after a suicide attempt and my life changed forever. I wrote my story (Fourth Step) and read it to my sponsor (Fifth Step), cried my eyes out and started healing from the inside out. Now I cry whenever I want because I'm grateful to feel EVERYTHING. It may not look like I am ok, but I am finally allowing myself to have real feelings. I no longer hide nor stuff feelings. If that makes me a cry baby, so be it! I've never felt healthier emotionally. So, I will hold on to Role 3 – Cry Baby.

"Keep your friends close,
but your enemies closer."

~ Mario Puzo

Me and Claudia

Chapter 5

Keeping My Friends Close

Looking back at my childhood and the beginning of my life as an adult, I never saw my feelings changing. People would always be staring because I would always be different in their eyes. It was very different in **my** eyes and my closest friends, however.

My oldest and dearest friend, Claudia, is my first memory of making a friend – a lifelong friend. Our parents bought brand new houses in a windy, small town in Northern California in what used to be mostly field, hence the name Fairfield. Our houses were two doors down from each other; another new house was between us. The community was built in a valley surrounded by dry, brown hills in the summer and green landscape in the winter. Our backyards were barren without landscaping or fences yet, as our houses were barely finished. There was a small retaining wall running the length of our block at the rear property line of our yards. Claudia and I happened to be in our own backyards one day and spotted each other right away. We both headed up our retaining walls, got to the top and walked toward each other meeting in the middle. We exchanged names and the inevitable question was next: "What happened to your arm?" I answered just like always: "I was born that way." I don't recall what we talked about after that, but Claudia ran home and told her mother she had met a new friend. She told me later she was excited and told her mom all about her new friend with "the hook". We were six years old and went all the way through school together until we both graduated from high school. We were more than best friends. We were family.

She would often forget about my arm when we were kids. She got new gloves once and I asked to try one on. She automatically tried to hand me the other one. I gave her an amused look and she said, "Oh, never mind!" We used to play "Jacks", an old game where we would sit on the floor, bounce a little ball, pick up a jack, then two, then three and catch the ball in time. Most kids would put the jacks in the other hand after they were picked up making it possible to catch the ball in that hand. Claudia asked me why I was using one hand to do it all. Again..."oh never mind!" Other kids would forget occasionally too. Maybe because I never made it a big deal or didn't use it as an excuse to not participate. I never wanted to think or act as if I was different from anyone else. Therefore, it became a shock and sometimes a slap in the face when the opportunity for reality would set in later in life. My biggest fear was never feeling comfortable in my own skin without something or someone to remind me that I wasn't. There always seemed to be a reminder when meeting new people, going to unfamiliar places, or trying on clothes. The feeling that always followed was: "There it is again – I almost forgot!"

I can't talk about best friends without mentioning Lorri – the one from my airport story. We met as freshmen in high school. Aside from our previously mentioned similarities (our names, birthdates and mutual interests) we are bonded by history and have always felt like part of each other's families. How did I get so lucky to have two best friends for five decades? What started as a teenaged, boy crazy, coming of age relationship has become an unconditional friendship with an unmatched mutual respect. We may not agree on some things like religion and politics, but it has never affected our tight bond. And like with my bestie, Claudia, we have remained as close as we have always been despite the different directions our lives have taken us.

Lorri has always addressed my arm differently than everyone else, however. It's her helpful approach I find absolutely endearing. If I'm struggling with a Ziplock bag, she gently takes it out of my hand, opens it for me and hands it back. She does things like this all the time without either of us talking about it. It's not because she thinks I can't do certain things myself. I see it as her wanting to just make life easier for me for a brief second. It's about her kind heart – without judgment – without drawing attention to these types of situations. I say, "thank you." She says, "you're welcome" and we go about our day. It's just "us." If I had to answer the question of who the most self-less person I know is – it's my little red-haired girlfriend, Lorri.

"The things that make me different are the things that make ME."

~ A.A. Milne

1991 Prosthesis with harness

Chapter 6

Keeping My Enemies Closer

Life has been hard for me, not just physically, but mostly mentally. There were times I felt like jumping out of my body into someone else's. A LOT of times. I heard someone once say, "I didn't just want to be like her. I wanted to BE her." I can't ever remember **not** feeling that way. It was hard for me to forget I was different when there were constant reminders. Children can often be cruel when they don't understand.

There was a boy who went to the same elementary school I did – the neighborhood bully. Danny would ride his bicycle by our house and yell, "HEY CAPTAIN HOOK!" One day the first graders were lined up on the stairs leading into our classrooms after recess. Danny began taunting me by calling me names; specifically the clever one he thought only he had discovered. It was the favorite label given to me by kids that didn't know me. I kicked him as hard as I could. The teacher sent us both to the principal's office. Mr. Dillon addressed me first. "Laura, why did you kick Danny?" With my tail between my legs, crying, and thinking about how much more trouble I would be in when my parents found out, I answered "HE CALLED ME CAPTAIN HOOK!" The principal dismissed me and I could hear Danny being paddled on the way back to my class.

In that moment I realized that words could hurt me far worse than falling from my bike and skinning both knees. I also felt powerful at the same time because someone actually protected me. Although it didn't heal my heart or change the fact that I was different, it made me special for a moment. I certainly didn't feel better than anyone, but feeling special instead of less than was a slight improvement.

It took a long time to be comfortable in my own skin. I learned to hide my hurt by disguising it with sarcasm or angry responses. One of my first boyfriends took me on a date to the local county fair. I was so proud to be on a real date with a young man who could drive. William was tall, good looking and had great hair – long, dark and like an actor. It was the 70's after all and that was important! My dad hated him, however. He worked as a junk man, drove an old beat-up Chevy truck and my father thought he could change his t-shirt more often, but more importantly have a better job than salvaging car parts.

Nevertheless, I was 16 and allowed to go on a date finally. I felt like a grownup. We walked around the fairgrounds for a while. I don't think he could afford to go on any of the thrill rides or play carnival games, but I didn't mind. We got a refreshment to cool off from this perfect, hot day and sat down on a small, grassy area next to a snack stand. There was no one else in the world. Just us enjoying time together eating our ice creams. A little boy who looked to be between eight and ten years old started his approach. He slowly walked in our direction as he stared at me with his mouth wide open. We watched him circle us and waited for the inevitable question, "WHAT HAPPENED TO YOUR ARM?" I can still hear his gasp before he spoke. I thought he was old enough to know better. Didn't his parents teach him any manners? How dare he interrupt our secluded moment and remind me that I would never get to just be left alone (like everyone else). I answered in a matter-of-fact tone with the first thing that came to mind. "Well, one day I got so hungry I ate it." I was satisfied and amused with my comeback. It took the edge off my anger. Although I didn't crack a smile, I thought it was funny if not clever. Until I saw his reaction, that is. He covered his wide-open mouth with his hand, sucked in air with a gasp and ran away. I felt so awful I wanted to cry. I didn't know if I felt worse that I was singled out as the freak at the fair or because I had become a bitter, sarcastic, mean young lady who could terrorize a child. I did not want to be her. I just wanted to be left alone if I couldn't be someone else. Anyway, a hard lesson learned, I never did that again.

One day my daughter's little friend from across the street came over. We called our neighbors across the street "The Burbs", as they resembled the odd family from the 1989 movie starring Tom Hanks. It's not because we thought they were the suspected ritualistic murderers in the film. They were more eclectic and unusual. We lived in a small housing tract in a suburban area. There were children's toys everywhere and garbage strewn around their front yard where long stalks of corn grew. We also wondered why the entire family was covered in what appeared to be blue ink. We learned the father worked in a plant that manufactured blue, drop-in, cleaning tablets for toilets. We never knew them personally so we just renamed them the Smurfs because of their acquired skin color and the abundance of children. We rarely saw the parents, but there seemed to be blue children everywhere.

I was outside washing my car in the driveway. Our daughter, Michelle, was also outside playing in our yard. One of the Smurfs, who was younger than Michelle, came across the street. She asked her a question – a new one I had never heard before. "Michelle, why does your mom have a machine on her arm?" I don't know what the answer was because I dropped the hose and ran into our house.

The difference between how I reacted then as opposed to how I would today is simple. Back then I was in my late 20's. I was still self-conscious about my arm even though I thought I had come to terms with my dissimilarity. It wasn't the question at all. If the same situation presented itself today, I would have answered it instead of expecting my daughter to. I remember exactly how I felt over 30 years ago and why. This brilliant question from this child was not one I hadn't heard before, but rather asked in such a unique manner. I laugh about it today because she said "machine" when in fact it was! She recognized my arm as a device that functioned with a hook and cables. Out of the mouths of babes! The reason the question struck an emotional chord with me was because it was the first time I remember hearing it as a mother. I thought, "Great. This question is always going to be there no matter how old I am or what generation comes along." I was still young and had so many unresolved feelings about EVERYTHING; not just my prosthetic life. I was never going to be *normal*. I was never going to feel comfortable dressed up or in a swimsuit. The first thing anyone would ever notice would be my arm - not my clothes or how I looked in a swimsuit. Looking back now it wasn't all that bad! The real issue was how I felt at my core at that time. It took many, many years to accept and love myself as I am, but not because my first husband told me to!

It has taken far too many years to rid myself of bitter sarcasm, but I'm sure most everyone has had hard lessons to learn. I know I'm not that unique, and even if you don't relate, I am aware that my most valuable lessons came with hard knocks, particularly because of my unrealistic expectations as a child.

People have asked me what I would change if I had the opportunity. The ***If only*** scenario...My answer is always "nothing" after I shut the voice up in my head that says, "I wish I had two hands". Every good and bad decision has made me who I am today. Let's face it – I am a product of my experiences. I wouldn't change being married four times. Husband #1 and #2, Danny (not the bully from grammar school), gave me a daughter who blessed me with the most precious gift of my granddaughter. Husband #3, Charles, was also a blessing even though the marriage only lasted a year. He did two things in that short amount of time: 1) He made it easier to finally end the marriage that failed twice, and 2) I would have never met Husband #4, the love of my life, if I hadn't been so unhappy with myself for choosing the wrong partner again. Not to mention the sadness I still feel when I think about hurting him by not loving him enough. It just wasn't fair to him at all. My family wondered if I would live a normal life after I was born different. That really meant my getting married and having children – the epitome of what a woman was supposed to do in the 50's. Well, I showed them! As usual – the kind of overachiever I never wanted to be.

If only I knew what I wanted to be when I grew up sooner. *If only I hadn't* wasted my professional career by not realizing my true passion of writing. If I could keep my current life, family, friends and still follow my dreams of traveling when we retire, I might only change that one thing, but only under those conditions. My parents always told me I could do anything. I wasn't allowed to say, "I can't". I was spanked when I did something wrong. I was scolded for cutting the corner too close in the hallway to my room. Evidence of chipped paint by a stainless-steel hook was proof of my poor navigation. I can't tell you how many times I heard, "WHY CAN'T YOU BE MORE CAREFUL?" I got in trouble for accidentally dropping things and heard "LAURA, SLOW DOWN" and "HURRY UP AND GET THOSE DISHES DONE" simultaneously. I was grounded for cutting school, smoking cigarettes and being disrespectful with the typical teenage back talk. If my parents did anything right, treating me no differently than a child with two hands was it. What they forgot to tell me was that I was limited in career choices. Oh – and putting a fitted sheet on a waterbed was impossible for me. Ah, the memories from the 70's!

My father put together a binder called My Interests. I think I was around 10 years old, maybe in fourth or fifth grade. The project had different subjects tabbed off in sections with blank paper for my essays. The tabs were labeled with things like My Favorite President, Where do I Want to Go, and What Do I Want to Be When I Grow Up. Some of the essays required research from an encyclopedia. Computers and the World Wide Web hadn't been discovered yet. All my reports were handwritten. I was so proud of my work that I saved that completed binder until I got married - the first time! I loved working on it! So why did I write about being a stewardess? I know - they're called flight attendants now. The point is I knew I wanted to write over 50 years ago!

All I ever wanted to be was a homemaker with at least two children, but I had professional aspirations as backup plans throughout the years of growing up. The one lasting the longest was veterinarian. I took all college preparation classes in high school because I wanted to enroll at U.C. Davis. That is, until I figured out a vet needs two hands to hold a cat's mouth open, or for simple procedures like taking temperatures and obviously more complicated issues like surgery.

The next bright idea was becoming a dental assistant. Our high school offered training through the Regional Occupational Program (R.O.P.). My friend, Lorri and I signed up because it was 15 credits, and we wouldn't have to physically be at the high school during the last semester of our senior year. My internship, or on the job training, was at the Mare Island Naval Shipyard in Vallejo, California. Being used to new people having a perplexed look when meeting for the first time, I didn't give the strange looks a second thought. Eventually, a female dental assistant who worked there fulltime said, "Shouldn't you find something else to do? Dental assisting requires two hands and you're not fast enough". I was heartbroken - not because she had the nerve to say that to me, but because it was true. So, I screwed the male dental assistant who was training me a few times, somehow made it through the program, and graduated high school by the skin of my teeth. ***If only*** my parents had prepared me for the inevitable. There would be things I shouldn't do even if I could. Being unaware of future obstacles only caused disappointment and anger when certain tasks became unsuccessful.

"You own everything that happened to you. Tell your stories. If people wanted you to write warmly about them, they should've behaved better."

~ Anne Lamott

Michelle (middle) and her parents
John and me (left) Danny and Kathy (right)

Chapter 7

Feelings...Nothing More Than Feelings

According to the American Psychological Association, "anger is an emotion characterized by antagonism toward someone or something you feel has deliberately done you wrong. Anger can be a good thing. It can give you a way to express negative feelings, for example, or motivate you to find solutions to problems. But excessive anger can **cause** problems. Unleashing anger doesn't produce the sense of catharsis people crave. It tends to feed on itself instead."

When a person's feelings are hurt, the area of the brain responsible for the affective component of pain is activated. I believe there's a difference in the kind of anger from someone cutting me off in traffic than the type of anger caused by someone's word or actions toward me. In my case, anger has typically been my hurt feelings.

Per Kay Kosak Abrams, Ph.D. in her article ***First Comes Hurt, Then Comes Anger and Aggression, Washington Parent Magazine, January 2003:*** "To understand and manage angry feelings and aggressive behavior, we must first recognize and remember that anger comes from hurt. Aggression is the behavioral response – the acting on the hurt and anger. Empathy is the curative response that eases the hurt so we can shore up our coping defenses."

To this day I can still be overly sensitive in certain situations whether they are related to my difference or not. I still hate being teased. I still want to be liked by everyone even if I have no reason for desiring them in my life in any capacity. It feels like being the last one picked for the team in a P.E. class. Surely, I can be worthy if everyone else likes me.

Being stared at by others was my first glimpse of anger/hurt feelings as a child. This feeling has followed me into my adult life and is measured by what mood I happen to be in at the time, if I'm too tired, hungry, or how much sleep I got the night before.

As a child, I felt anything from, "Why me? Will I ever be good enough? Haven't parents taught their children it's rude to stare? Shouldn't adults know better?" to "Why can't I be done with this already?" What I know isn't always how I feel or my first reaction to being singled out in the room. It often feels like I am the main attraction for a side show. Maybe that's why I hate circuses.

The fact is there will always be ignorance and I have learned to be empathetic. What started out as others' curiosity, fear, and the need to learn more about my situation, became something much bigger for me than I had imagined.

All my feelings of inadequacy, belief that I was less than or less valuable than anyone caused a domino effect of bad behaviors. I constantly looked for ways to fill the empty void inside that was directly caused by a lack of self-love. My secret desire has always been to start life over as someone else.

Was I shy or did I crave attention? I have recently concluded that I am both shy as well as one who craves attention. How is this possible? I always thought the answer had to be one or the other. Understanding that I am not terminally unique has led me to believe I have always been shy. I have never craved attention because I never wanted to be noticed. I have NEVER wanted to be the center of attention. I never wanted to be "noticed" nor did I ever want a spot light on me. Remember? I was the little girl who wanted people to stop staring at her. I was the teenager who wanted to be like everyone else. I was the high school student who wanted to be a part of the group because I was like them, not because I was different than them. How could I become both the person who wants to be seen as an equal while knowing I'm not. I couldn't do something as simple as clapping my hands, but went through the motions anyway trying to avoid drawing attention to myself. I can't count the number of times I've caused bruises in the palm of hand pretending to clap with my hook.

Well, if you asked me then, I would have told you I was shy. Afraid of EVERYTHING. Today I would tell you that was true. I was afraid. Afraid of being judged. Afraid of the next time I didn't measure up to everyone else. Afraid of boys not ever finding me attractive or worthy of a real relationship or future. Afraid of never having the fairy tale: Marrying the man of my dreams, having children and being Mrs. Cleaver. After all, that wasn't asking much in my own mind. As I was maturing, women wanted careers, independence, a life that didn't depend on a man if need be. All I wanted was to be a better mother than mine, to have a husband who loved me more than ANYTHING else (unlike my father who never knew love at all) and to be someone else because I never felt worthy of having any of my dreams come true. EVER. Somebody call a WAHMBULANCE!

Meanwhile it was a fight to appear as if I had no fear. How does one do that? It was always an inside job for me - an inside struggle or tug of war. Not to mention how I wanted everyone else to "see" me as "normal" because of what I wanted to project: confidence, being as good as everyone else, but not feeling that way myself (while feeling inept because of it). So, I remained confident on the outside while feeling tormented on the inside.

Don't get me wrong. I did crave attention as a child at the same time as feeling shy. Admiration for overcoming obstacles, or a job well done was a great feeling. Everyone should feel successful after a great accomplishment. It was the internal conflict of meeting challenges and defeating difficult or impossible obstacles for myself while knowing the result was subpar. My peers seemed to easily face and overcome these challenges. I tried to remain normal to people who effortlessly participated in day-to-day activities without having to learn, feel or think twice about activities such as catching a softball and trying to figure out how to throw it back in two motions instead of three. But when I learned how to complete a task as a challenged person, honestly, I did expect a little more credit! After all, I worked harder to achieve the ultimate result and GODDAMMIT I deserve extra credit! Yet, I never wanted to feel special, deserving or more entitled because of my "difference". So, am I supposed to feel proud, or guilty for feeling anything more than the person who worked so hard to achieve the feeling of accomplishment?

Yes, I was shy. Yes, I craved attention. Doesn't everyone?! HA! Especially after one has felt the honor, acknowledgment, or praise and reward. I am still no different than anyone else, am I? Some may crave attention because they want to be the most important in the room. Some may want the attention but are too shy to take it to that place. The answer to this question is far different for each person, more complicated than it looks (it's not simple or recognizable for some), but it is a great question for people who choose or want to acknowledge what is an honest, deep-felt, heart driven answer. This is a question that applies to anyone; not just to those of us who have an obvious answer regarding challenges we face in life.

The answer was always "NOT ME" when the question of who loved me was asked. There were many, many times I thought no one else really loved me. I'd like to go back and shake that child, young woman and middle-aged lady who struggled and judged herself mostly by her exterior shell. Inevitably, that outer shell became older, more wrinkled with imperfections appearing as moles and age spots. A kind woman once told me, "THEY'RE SUN SPOTS, not AGE SPOTS!" I liked that!

I never thought it would happen. Actually, I knew it would happen. Just not overnight. The reflection I see every day shocks me every single time. What I see is not how I feel. At. All.

I feel young. My skin *feels* soft and smooth. My eyes *feel* bright, cheery and wrinkle-free. Where did all the gray hair come from? How did my neck hold out so long only to betray me with sagging pockets on each side of my chin and wrinkly, loose skin hanging below the jaw line? And why won't my nose stop growing?! I barely recognize the woman staring back at me. Who is she?

I'll tell you who I think she is. She is imperfect from the inside out. The woman I see has only recently learned who she is. She went to difficult schools most of her life beginning with how to be an only child who was different, and being raised by imperfect parents. Here was an insecure, flawed and inadequate little girl who had no clue how much harder life would become. She couldn't wait to get older, finish school, meet her knight in shining armor, have her own children raised differently than she was and give them opportunities she wasn't afforded. Life would be so much easier if she could just be a grownup, find true love and be the best mother ever. She had so much to learn.

Looking back is never easy. Today I may see someone older in my reflection, but I like her. I am proud of who she has become despite the directions she took to get there. She is a good wife who still makes mistakes but scratched her way through the ruble of difficult relationships to find "the one" who taught her to love herself first. She is a good mother; not the best, but she certainly has done her best with all she had. It's all anyone can expect, isn't it?

The woman in the mirror is happy today. She loves herself, is confident sometimes, secure in who she is inside and is still figuring out her purpose in this world. She gets up every day hoping to be a better version of herself, kinder than yesterday, hopefully smarter, or at least wiser, and looking forward to her dreams coming true. She hopes to be a better wife, mother, and grandmother than the day before. She hopes to wake up every day with even more wrinkles and gray hair because the alternative is much worse. The reflection is older, but inside she is someone who wants to live to see another day. Life is hard, but life is good.

"Embrace what makes you different."

~ Timothy Q. Mouse

(from the movie, Dumbo)

Left – 1964 Disneyland

Middle – 2008 50th birthday at Disney World

Right – 2019 LauraSue's family at Disneyland

Chapter 8

My Happy Place

I can still remember the excitement and preparation for our annual vacation to Disneyland. My parents would buy me new clothes and sneakers before the trip. I'm sure my new shorts outfits had more to do with not fitting into the prior year's wardrobe rather than just getting new clothes for vacation. Nonetheless, it meant a Disneyland vacation was in store for me.

The drive was long - about 450 miles and eight hours of travel time before I-5 was finished. My dad made it in about 5 ½ hours after the new interstate opened and only stopped for gas once. I remember that being a big deal at the time because of V-8 engines. We would leave at 5:00 a.m., while it was still dark, and watched the sun come up along the way. I was always too excited to sleep the night before or in the car most times. We would try and imitate the faces that semi-trucks seemed to have made with their grills and headlights. The truck antennae gave them even more personality. Some looked mean, while others resembled little kids with cute or surprised expressions. I remember one year counting Volkswagen Bugs all the way to Anaheim to keep occupied. Obviously, this was way before DVD players in the car, tablets and cell phones. My job was to spot the Matterhorn before we could take the exit to our motel – always within walking distance to the Magic Kingdom. The feeling of "being there" was euphoric. One year, my dad drove straight to the Disneyland parking lot so we could be there right when the Park opened. All the other times we would go directly to the motel, rest (against my will, of course) and go to Knott's Berry Farm the next morning. We always saved Disneyland for the second day so Knott's wouldn't be a major disappointment. Like I couldn't remember from the previous year?!

Wikipedia describes Knott's Berry Farm as "a world-renowned theme park built from the humblest beginnings. What started as a small berry farm soon began to grow into a family themed park destination thanks to famous fried chicken dinners, boysenberries and an Old West Ghost Town. Knott's now bursts with attractions and entertainment for all ages, including first class roller coasters, stage shows, interactive experiences, delicious food creations and family-friendly fun featuring Snoopy and the Peanuts Gang. The once small family farm has grown into today's family fun destination."

Back in the 60's and 70's there weren't many rides. There were trains, make believe gun fights, Old West shows and exhibits. You could have souvenir chalk drawings done of yourself by artists to commemorate visits there, or eat good food from take-out to a southern style fried chicken café or a fine steakhouse. I remember Knott's Berry Farm as a fun place, but I think it was more tolerable because Disneyland would be the next day. Although the Farm was a stepping stone to my happy place, I could've easily bypassed this part of vacation. It did create more excitement knowing I had something bigger and better to look forward to though. Especially, after this park eventually offered more rides providing better adrenaline rushes!

The second day of vacation always began rising early and going to breakfast. We would get to the park as it was opening, buy our tickets and get in line at the turnstiles.

I still get a little choked up when I get the first glimpse of the Disneyland Railroad which sits above a Mickey Mouse flower bed, but even more so walking through the tunnel onto Main Street.

There is still a plaque above one of the tunnels that reads, "Here you leave today and enter the world of yesterday, tomorrow and fantasy". This quote from Walt Disney himself always reminds me that this is my happy place. Here I have not a worry in the world. I am sure other children feel excitement as well as anticipation of fun rides, character visits with photos, a sense of adventure, exploration and wonder – a place where kids can be kids. For me, it's all of those things and more.

Disneyland has always been the one place I am unaware of other children or adults staring at me because of my arm. They are much too busy discovering this beautiful Land. They are smelling freshly made popcorn, coffee and breakfast being cooked as they enter the Park. They are taking in the first glimpse of Sleeping Beauty's castle and listening to the cable car bells ringing while horses are clomping down Main Street. Disneyland is the one place I can leave my difference behind and be unaware of attracting anyone's unwanted attention. I am also too busy being happy to think about who else I'd rather be.

I remember wanting to live there as a child. As a teen it grew into wishing I could work there. I continued to go every year as an adult until later when life got in the way. I have been over 50 times and have enjoyed it as much every time. I have been fortunate to see Walt Disney's creation through my own daughter's eyes and now through my granddaughter's. Seeing Disneyland in a completely different light was something I never saw coming.

My life changed the moment I became a grandmother. Who knew a heart had so much more room for love? My heart was full when my daughter Michelle was born. Until now she was the only one I would walk in front of a bus for if it meant saving her. She has to share that scenario now with her daughter, LauraSue.

I remember fantasizing about sharing my happy place with the three most important people of my life almost immediately. Although I had already experienced Disneyland with John and Michelle, I had no idea how differently I would feel seeing my favorite place in the world through my granddaughter's eyes. LauraSue had already been exposed to The Mickey Mouse Clubhouse on TV, Disney themed merchandise, movies and a "little" (tongue placed firmly in cheek) influence by her Nonnie (me).

The preparation began just before LauraSue turned three years old. We primed her with Mickey Mouse, Sleeping Beauty's castle, and stories of Disneyland. Her mother (Michelle), father (Brian) and half-brother (Little Brian) joined us in the SUV Brian rented to make our journey more comfortable. I bought matching t-shirts, backpacks, mouse ears and hats for our trip. The road trip included games to pass the time; i.e., a piece of Velcro strewn across the front seats with a car stuck to it. Every time Brian would tell us we traveled 50 miles, Little Brian would get to move the car to the next marker to visualize how much closer we were to Anaheim. Then, of course, I passed on the tradition of looking for the Matterhorn before taking the exit off Interstate 5.

One of my fondest memories is all of us walking through the turnstiles and anticipating what was on the other side of the tunnels below the railroad. It wasn't about me anymore, however. There is something to be said about the spiritual principle from Alcoholics

Anonymous, "You can't keep it unless you give it away". LauraSue's first walk down Main Street brings a smile to my face every time I think about it. "LauraSue...do you see the castle?" She leaned up from her stroller, pointed her finger toward the castle and said, "I SEE IT!!!" Every emotion I have ever felt about Disneyland changed in that moment. The tears in my eyes and smile on my face said it all. My granddaughter's excitement and her being able to experience something so important to me was priceless.

Although Disneyland is not as much as an escape for me anymore, it is still my happy place and represents the most important coping mechanism of my life. Being able to share it with my granddaughter was a bonus.

> "It's never too late to live happily ever after."
>
> ~ Unknown

Me, mother and father

Chapter 9

Parenting

No Judgment
It Just Is

My hopes and dreams changed as I learned what was achievable and, most importantly, possible in my own mind. I can't speak to good or bad parenting. I don't claim to know anything about being a mother. I can't place blame on anyone now that I know my own personal best was based on what I knew and the willingness to heal, learn more and change to the best of my ability. It has been a huge undertaking, an inside job and not for the squeamish. I do know my parents told me I was able to do everything. I wasn't allowed to say, "I can't". I can't, however, imagine how my life would be today had they NOT taught me to be independent and try everything. They taught me to have hope.

My parents guided me in a positive way when it came to my birth defect and never allowed me to give up. Although there were obstacles in my life, I would never have found out how much was possible without trying. Failures and successes came to fruition by effort, persistence, and most times hard work. Most achievements happened because each lesson learned made it easier to learn another. For example: Once I learned to tie my shoes, or different knots, knitting and crocheting became attainable. Learning to play keyboards paved the way for playing a guitar. The same idea is true for most other functions as well. I'm looking forward to clapping my hands, feeling hot in one hand and cold in the other if there is another life after this one though!

It would be a lie if I didn't tell you, the reader, the entire truth. Were my parents the best? Not even close. Did I love them both? Absolutely - even to the point of believing my parents should be the envy of all my friends. My immediate family was close-knit and always embraced when saying hello and goodbye. Extended family gathered in a park for annual family reunions where about 300 people gathered. I genuinely felt proud of my family. How disappointing it was to find out the actual truth while reflecting as an adult.

A friend of mine once told me, "Your dad doesn't know everything, Laura." I do not recall my response, but it was probably something defensive like, "I KNOW THAT", but it hadn't occurred to me to believe otherwise. My father was manipulative, convincing, self-righteous, and dangerously charming. I was convinced he was more intelligent than most because he told me so. My school girlfriends used to tell me how handsome he was which originally made me feel proud. That is, until I learned there were more important labels to place on people. Unfortunately, I hadn't fully understood "Beauty is only skin-deep" from a poem written by Sir Thomas Overbury called <u>A Wife.</u> After all, my father always placed more emphasis on someone's physical appearance - especially how one dressed. I will describe him as a narcissist, temperamental, a liar and just plain mean. He could also be very loving and affectionate. Therein lies my confusion.

I choose not to give my father much more attention. I sure as hell won't dedicate much more time to him for the purpose of my story. In short, he disowned me twice: 1). for marrying a Black man, 2). for divorcing the same husband after a year and "turning the whole family upside down". I can't imagine cutting my only daughter out of my life and telling her, "My life is a lot happier without you in it". Still, I forgave him (for me) and temporarily moved forward with our relationship by only keeping him at arm's length. My therapist at the time offered a pretty good solution. She said, "Forgiving him doesn't mean you have to give him a front seat in your life." We stopped talking in July of 2014, when I went away for our annual Independence Day with my husband's family in Clear Lake, California. I sent my father a card for his birthday with a gift certificate explaining we were out of town and we wanted to continue his celebration when we returned home. I called when we got back, he didn't come to the phone, never called me back and neglected to thank me for the gift card. He chose to hold a grudge because I didn't bother to call him on his birthday despite my other acknowledgements. No, my parents weren't perfect, but it doesn't mean I can't remove toxic people from my life. It turns out I am the one much happier without him in mine.

My mother was also attractive. My father told me that was one of the reasons he married her. The other reason being she was the only one who "said no". She was a sulker. My father was a leaver. She fought back with being a screamer, martyr and lacked communication skills. Both of my parents lacked that skill. I didn't have a chance in Hell! I had to get those tools from a different toolbox. Even with her shortcomings, I would describe her as funny, compassionate in her own way and most importantly, unconditionally loving. For instance, instead of shutting me out, she explained how concerned she was that I was complicating my life with an interracial marriage. She said, "I don't agree with your decision, but I love you anyway". She wasn't a hugger and was the first to pull away from displays of affection, but I learned later it didn't mean she didn't feel.

My mom passed away on December 1, 1994, after an 18-year battle with lung cancer. She was diagnosed my senior year of high school – the year that was also to mark when my father would divorce her for good. Unfortunately, he didn't finally leave her in peace until they had been married 27 years (eight more years). That is when I finally got to know her. We did have a strained relationship for a while because I couldn't control her emotions for her, expected her to GET OVER IT ALREADY, and quite frankly didn't understand how much she loved my father. I will regret this part of our relationship forever, but am grateful I got to say this to her before she died: "Mom, I know you did the best you could. I know you must've heard I thought you were a bad mother, but you weren't. I also want you to know that I know exactly who my father is, and I love you". She couldn't respond with a respirator down her throat but nodded her head with tears in her eyes. She understood. We developed a good relationship after that one-sided hospital conversation and all those years I wasted not understanding her. She was funny when she decided to be my friend alongside being my mother.

One of the best memories of my mom was when we came home from shopping one day to find her house full of flies. My mother had a huge dislike for the insect. So, she grabbed a fly swatter immediately. She landed each hit with the precision of a professional pool player sinking each ball perfectly. Hoping her job was accomplished, she asked me if I saw any more. I looked up at the florescent light in the kitchen where at least a dozen flies were hanging out. I pointed up at them and gave my mother "a look". She yelled, "Who let all these fucking flies in here?!!" It was the first time in my life that I heard her use that word. You see...She hated it as much as her dislike for flies. Neither word was allowed in our house, especially at the dinner table. I found it both ironic and hysterical both things were happening at the same time. I started laughing, fell out of the kitchen chair and rolled on the floor. I think she was shocked that word escaped from her mouth too. She started openly laughing and said, "that felt good!"

The worst memory I have of my mother is the last night she was alive. I brought her home from the hospital after she had received intravenous antibiotics for an infection. I walked her inside her apartment and was unsure whether to stay or go home. She must've sensed it because she took my face into her hands and told me to go home and take care of my family. I didn't know she wasn't ok as she had told me. I also didn't know it would be the last time I would see her alive. I wish I would've stayed to help her transition. More importantly, I wish I had the opportunity to spend more quality filled years with my mother. There are still so many questions I need to ask her about life and being a woman. Unbeknownst to me she could have been the only one to understand my feelings about being a less than perfect mother myself.

"Nothing ever goes away until it has taught us what we need to know."

~ Pema Chodron

My grandparents - Paternal (left) and Maternal (right)

Chapter 10

Patterns that Built Me

My difference was still able to rear its ugly head even though my parents treated it appropriately and taught me well in that respect. Self-consciousness, low self-worth and being uncomfortable in my own skin was my own shit.

I used to hide my arm behind my back when I was a child. I began noticing people staring at me once I was aware of being different. It was much easier to conceal it rather than deal with all the gawking, rude questions and unwanted attention from strangers.

My aunt, my father's youngest sister, took me for a walk to the store one day when I was a child. A man was staring at me and I asked her why. She said "How do you know he's looking at you if you're not looking at him?" I see it as a brilliant response. It was a true statement.

My aunt doesn't see it as a great response and is shocked she actually came up with an answer on the fly. She really didn't know what to do or say and ended up locked in her room crying after we got home.

I learned very early in life that I could run and hide from just about anything I didn't want to deal with. The escaping mechanism of running was used by my parents as a coping skill as well.

My parents fought as long as I can remember. I never witnessed them problem solving or even engaging in healthy discussions of any kind. I don't say this to place blame on either one of them. They both came from vastly different worlds. I don't recall my mother's parents talking about anything much less fighting about it.

My maternal grandfather stayed silent – he was a quiet gentleman who probably thought it was just easier to let my grandmother rule the roost. He chose peace over confrontation with anyone; especially her. I believe that's the reason my mother never expressed feelings whether she was angry or sad. She sulked to illustrate displeasure or maybe to punish my father for hurting her. I rarely saw her break out in hysterical laughter either. To this day I only have one picture of her with a big, happy smile.

My father's parents communicated in a totally opposite fashion. My high-strung, Spanish grandmother was an emotional, demonstrative, and temperamental disciplinarian. My Mexican grandfather was the stern but quiet one. All he had to do was stand up from a chair to raise awareness and express his disapproval.

Both sets of grandparents were as different as night and day, as were my parents. My mother would shut down and hide while my father would throw a tantrum and leave. He would sometimes leave temporarily, but several times found another place to live. I don't remember how many times my parents separated before finally throwing in the towel after 27 years of marriage.

I thought every little girl I would meet would be like my best friend, Claudia. Maybe because she was the first real friend I ever had. I don't recall having any friends in kindergarten. My first school was in a different town about nine or ten miles away. It wasn't until beginning first grade that I remember having acquaintances, life-long friends, friends who haven't remained in my life, and of course, the bullies.

Claudia was and still is a tough act for anyone to follow. She is the first friend I trusted with my secrets, thoughts and feelings. Although I can remember always feeling self-conscious of my arm, she gave me hope that it wouldn't be a big deal for anyone - just me. I learned early on that the first question would always be, "What happened to your arm?" I also learned the responses to my answer, "I was born that way", would all be different and not everyone would like or love me anyway. How rude (a little sarcasm)! My first introduction to unconditional love was my Claudia. I still go to her when I want to "go home."

My biological family is quite a different story. I believe my mother's family was unusual and what some would call white trailer trash. One of my mother's sisters had eleven children (ten survived). Her younger daughters all resented me. One of my cousins told me why. Our grandmother bragged constantly about me. "You should see Laura play the organ and she only has one hand." She made sure they all knew how special she thought I was. Our grandmother even said, "She has a bedroom set just like Caroline Kennedy and I bought it for her." She actually bought it with money from an insurance policy she had opened for me and single handedly drained it! My cousins also didn't care for me much because they may have felt judged for living poorly, or maybe felt inferior or envious because of what I had. I was an only child after all. Whatever their reasons, we were never close.

My mother's other sister went from one man to another while leaving her three daughters with my grandparents. My grandparents also raised one of my cousin's two children as well. Their mother left them to go rogue and play leaving the responsibility of parenting to our grandparents for days at a time. Again, I'm not judging. I am not qualified, as I am also imperfect in the decisions I have made. I'm just trying to paint a picture of where I came from. When I saw Robin Williams interviewing Sally Fields for a nanny position in <u>Mrs. Doubtfire</u>, I lost it! <Screaming> "LAYLA GET BACK IN YOUR CELL - DON'T MAKE ME GET THE HOSE!" That was kind of like that side of my family.

The cherry (no pun intended) on top of this crazy bunch was my maternal grandmother. She actually set me up with her favorite "friend of the family". My mother used to play with him when they were children. He was 15 years older than me and previously tried out for this position with my cousins. My grandmother actually said, "It's your turn – I want him in the family". She carefully set up reasons for us to be together: A Bing Crosby Pro-am golf tournament, Grand National Rodeo Show, a San Francisco 49er vs. Los Angeles Rams game at Candlestick Park in San Francisco - just to name a few. I lost my virginity to him in the front seat of his Volkswagen at a golf tournament at Silverado Resort in Napa, California at the age of 15. Fortunately, I came to my senses as a freshman in high school who knew she was too young to even think about marrying anyone.

My father's family fell apart after my grandfather passed away. It seemed like the tight-knit family I was so proud of was not reality at all. Maybe I wasn't paying attention. Maybe the truth, lack of loyalty and their actual characters were kept from me. Maybe the glue holding my father, uncle and two aunts together was my grandparents. Whatever it was, all respect left with my grandfather only to be replaced with rudeness, hateful judgment of others, negativity and the like. Enter conditional love. As long as one lived life as they expected, you were in good. The moment you made a mistake or bad decision in their eyes, you were out!

Not only did they evolve with family situations, and hiding my difference from strangers, but my engrained patterns were also evident in my relationships. I married my first husband when I was 19 years old. We had a daughter after three years and divorced when she was eight months old. We ended up remarrying on our 5th wedding anniversary – same day, same place, same minister and same wedding rings. The minister said, "You kids look familiar". My dad said, "That's because you married them before and we're gonna do this again and again until you get it right"! We eventually divorced again after eight more years. I got remarried right after the divorce, but it only lasted less than two years. It is very clear to me that I *ran* from a long and difficult marriage to one that would never work either. So what did I do? I *ran* again...

I met the love of my life, best friend and soul mate while married to my third husband. We have been together ever since (30 years). I still run and/or shut down when we have a major conflict. After all these years I can't seem to change the pattern for good. I guess it will always be something I'll have to work on. It's really hard to change who I have been and what I have learned my whole life, but I refuse to give up despite reinventing myself over and over.

"Life does not have to be perfect to be wonderful."

~ Annette Funicello

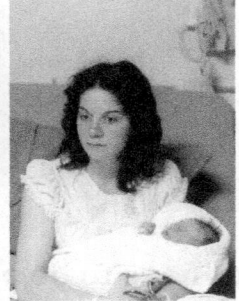

Michelle from beginning to present

Chapter 11

Motherhood – Not for the Squeamish

I suppose being forced to do things I didn't want to do is why I was more lenient to a fault with my own daughter. I never insisted she finish anything. She started tumbling and tap lessons as a toddler. As soon as the tumbling part of the program ended and tap began, she got bored, and we let her quit. Then she wanted to be in the elementary school band. So, we rented a clarinet. She didn't stick with that. Then she wanted to be on the drill team in middle school. She decided that also wasn't for her either after uniforms were purchased and going to training at Sacramento State College. I guess I didn't want to force her to do things if it wasn't fun. I felt, looking back now, hobbies like dance class, being a musician or anything else that takes dedication should be done because it is a passion. In hindsight I should have at least insist she stick with something long enough to hate it! She may have finished high school earlier instead of having to go back to school for a diploma in her 30's.

Michelle was conceived in love and planned...sort of. Her father, Danny, asked me if I was using a contraceptive on the night he returned from an Air Force temporary duty assignment (TDY). When I answered, "No", he responded with the statement, "Well, it's now or never". I am absolutely positive our daughter was created that night because we continued using protection until we learned I was pregnant.

Our daughter was born on January 1st at 6:34 a.m. She was the first baby born in upper Solano County for the new decade. We were interviewed by and displayed in two local newspapers and rewarded with gifts by downtown merchants. I was terrified. How could I be so happy, proud, ecstatic, and so terribly scared at the same time? How would I give her a bath? I envisioned her slipping out of my fingers and at the least being injured bouncing off the sides of the kitchen sink. I visualized stabbing her sides with diaper pins since I didn't have left fingers to prevent puncturing her delicate skin. My mother gave Michelle her first bath because she had the same fears, although she never expressed those concerns. I only learned how she felt after carrying resentments for years and wondering why she robbed me of this first milestone as a mother. She answered, "Because I didn't know if you could do it" when I finally asked her why she "took over my job." My hurt was replaced with empathy and compassion. This was the beginning of understanding who my mother was as only another mother could. We do the best we can with the tools we have.

I could write another memoir entirely about my role as a mother, my struggles, guilt, shame, fulfillment, happiness, feeling proud and loving my daughter with my entire being. Maybe sharing an assignment from college will allow me to convey some of these feelings to you – the reader. Some is still true at the time I wrote this. Some may not be. Nonetheless, it illustrates how I felt at the time.

Metaphor Paper
    Laura A. Kendall
    Philosophy 251, Critical Thinking
    May 30, 2001

Children and the Weather

I can remember the day my doctor informed my husband and I that we were expecting a child. Although I cannot remember exactly what the weather was like on that important day in May, I can remember how I felt. The day was like one with the most beautiful and perfect weather imaginable. The sun was just beginning to shine after a spring shower while a bright, colorful rainbow streaked across the sky. I felt wonderful, like a new woman with the warmth of the sun only shining on the new mother and father.

The sun shone on me for the remaining eight months. I never felt so happy, healthy and full of energy. Being pregnant was like preparing for a long vacation, not being exactly sure where you would be going and hoping for perfect weather.

We understood that clouds would have to roll in once in a while. We knew, as we were also children at one time, there would be rain. We hoped that there would be mostly sunshine, rainbows and crisp, cool breezes from the ocean.

Our daughter, Michelle, was born on New Year's Day in 1980. After 15 hours of hard, induced labor, broken blood vessels in my face, and hardly a breath left in my body, our baby had finally arrived. Although this new life came into this world like a tidal wave, she was as beautiful as an angel shining in the sun.

Michelle was a well-mannered, polite and charming little girl. We were so proud to have such a delightful daughter who spent weekends with family begging to take care of her. Our baby, the first niece, first grandchild and first great-grandchild had brought sunshine into our families' lives as well. Michelle's childhood was the calm before the storm.

"Teenagers are God's way of preparing for the empty nest" (author unknown). Our daughter reached puberty like the quiet before a tornado. Michelle stopped taking school seriously and rebelled in any way possible. The change in her attitude and demeanor did not begin gradually like sprinkles before a torrential rain. The full-blown storm began like an unexpected hurricane. The storm had taken away our sunshine.

We went to school conferences, helped her with homework, went to four different counselors and learned how best to communicate with Michelle. All our approaches would work temporarily. Then our daughter would regress back into the same behavior as if she preferred the storm to the sun.

Our daughter continues to ride the storm like on a boat lost at sea. The wind and rain beat on her, but she cannot find her way back to shore. The storm is too intense and she cannot feel sunshine long enough for warmth. Michelle sees glimpses of clear days and a rainbow now and then. Then more inclement weather takes my girl down before she can fully recover to enjoy what good weather feels like.

My baby is 21 years old now. She has been in juvenile hall, has never finished high school and is now homeless. I have rescued her from her private storm more times than I should have. Her father and I have decided to let the rain fall on our daughter. We are hoping that Michelle will become too cold, too wet and too miserable to stay in the terrible weather. We pray God will take care of our baby until she learns to take shelter from the rain. If we continue to give our daughter a raincoat, Michelle will never learn to appreciate how to stay out of the rain and enjoy the sunshine with the rest of the world.

Laura Kendall

University of Phoenix Online

I currently struggle with doing the right thing or feeling appropriately to live my own life to its fullest. After 40 years of being a good mother, bad mother, making the right decisions, beating myself up for bad ones, or worse, not having done anything at all, I am learning to let go. Yes, I still take back guilt, shame, and regret at times, but they are fewer and far between. If my mother taught me one thing it was, we all do the best we can. Our children do not come with instruction manuals. Even if they did, mothers would still be exempt from making mistakes. Especially when we have hearts that belong mostly to our babies.

My daughter will have to make her own choices and decisions. Her mother must get out of the way. When, and only when, Michelle decides to get out of her own way will things begin to shine again for everyone. I will never lose hope, but I will let go of things I can't control and give myself a break. I am not implying this is easy. All I want for her is to be happy. All I want for us is to be a happy, healthy family who spends quality time together. I refuse to lose hope, but more importantly, I will never give up on my daughter.

"The pivotal moments in your life are always made up of smaller pieces, things that seemed insignificant at time, but in fact brought you to where you needed to be."

~ Elizabeth Norris

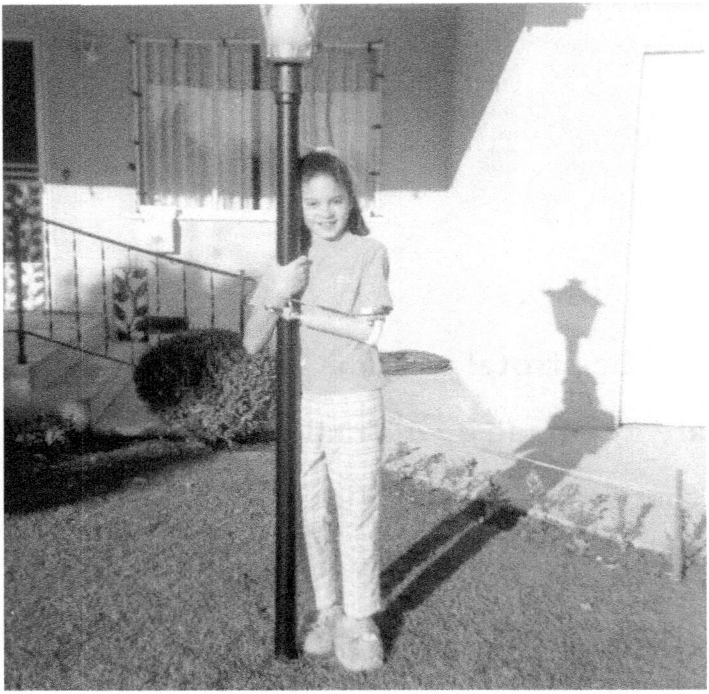

Chapter 12

Hands Down... The Most Pivotal Point in My Life

Some children have imaginary friends, security blankets or stuffed animals that serve as a transitional object. Psychologists believe these items help children feel relaxed while discovering the unfamiliar world outside of their home, love, and comfort zones. A security blanket was one of my comfort items and my thumb was its partner. One could not exist without the other.

My "blankey" was made of satin or silk over some kind of batting. I only know this because all that was left of it were parts of torn, soft, beige satin and ripped batting. My mother kept one piece of my blankey and gave it to me when I had my daughter. She had to cut it in four pieces so I would have one while the others were being washed.

She said I used to stand under the clothesline, sucking my thumb while waiting for my blanket to dry.

The inevitable time came for everyone to jump in and break *my* habit for *me*. My parents put Mercurochrome on my thumb to discourage me with the awful taste. Mercurochrome was used as an antiseptic for small cuts. It contained mercury as well as a red dye. The dye made it more difficult to detect inflammation or infection and it was taken off the shelves eventually. I began crying as soon as I put my thumb in my mouth. Then I immediately rubbed my eyes followed by screaming as the burning ensued. My grandfather came to the rescue, washed my hand and eyes, put my thumb back in my mouth for me, and said, "There. Now that's a good thumb."

Next, a husband of one of my aunt's, put a sock on my right hand and secured it with a rubber band. He knew I would be unable to get it off without a left hand while sleeping. I remember the sock looking dirty, but hopefully it was washed and just stained from use. I remember referring to it as "a dirty sock" over the years.

I can also remember waking up with a shriveled thumb as a teenager. Apparently, I continued this habit unconsciously in my sleep. I can't remember when sucking my thumb in the daytime ended, nor when the night-time habit stopped. I just know my thumb looks normal when I wake up now! Well, sort of.

My mother used to have a cedar chest when I was a toddler. It was open one day and I had to see what was in there. I peeked in, accidentally pulled the top down and smashed my thumb between the lid and base. My security thumb became wrapped up and inaccessible. So, I began sucking the stump on my left arm. My family thought it was funny because if you didn't know I was missing that hand, you would think the entire thing was in my mouth! Wish I had a picture of that to share!

For as long as I can remember, my oldest wish was having a hand, or as close to it as possible. My parents and the prosthetist repeatedly told me I had to wait until I stopped growing. And wait I did. For what seemed like an eternity. Surely, this would give me the break I needed. A break mainly needed from people staring and the never-ending question, "What happened to your arm?"

Hands down...the most pivotal point in my life was when I was 12 years old and my wish finally came true. I should have known how this would end! I went through a long transition every time I had to change prosthetics. No one likes change, but refitting and alterations made after growth periods or just plain wear and tear were especially difficult. Brand new prosthetics took many months of relearning and getting comfortable. More so than breaking in new shoes. Shoes are just uncomfortable, but we typically don't have to learn how to use new ones. Shoes all work the same way. They don't open and close, grip items or function by themselves. Some amputees never learn to use a prosthesis because it takes a lot of work/practice. They end up learning to use what they have left of their limbs, or other appendages, to function and complete certain tasks. I am considered a "user." I utilize my arms until there is nothing left of them. I was four years old when my prosthetist asked my mother, "How did Laura manage to bend a curved, stainless steel hook straight out. What used to resemble the Captain's hook was contoured into a straight, more sword-like configuration. I was being a normal kid and figuring out how to swing from one ring to another on the jungle gym (what we used to call monkey bars). I suppose the rings were a bit too far apart for me. I missed grabbing the next bar with my right hand and ended up hanging from the other ring by my hook. We learned stainless steel meant nothing as far as being durable in my world.

We also learned change involving a non-functioning prosthesis was even worse. This cosmetic hand was just that. I could detach the hook by unscrewing it from the prosthesis. Then I could screw the "hand" into place and voila! Instant hand-looking "thing." The fingers could be moved manually. In other words, I could bend the middle finger up and curl the others down to give someone the proverbial "bird". However, I could not grasp, pick up or hold anything. The hand was covered by a latex glove dyed to match the color of my real hand as closely as possible, but did not look real. At. All. I couldn't even live out my dream of wearing two gloves because the fingers didn't spread far enough apart to get a glove completely on. The only positive result of my life-long desire to have a "hand" was finally being somewhat incognito. The shiny, silver, eye-catching hook was gone. BUT I couldn't do anything. I would say it was worthless, but we did get some good laughs with it.

One time, back in middle school, my friends and I would have seances in my parent's front yard at night. We would all gather in a circle, hold hands (Claudia was always the one who held my hook in any situation like this), and proceed to call up the dead. This whole scenario was really about my holding hands with a boy from school that I had a crush on. We decided to play a trick on him. I stuffed newspaper inside the hand to the end of the glove, put ketchup inside it to resemble blood, and hid it in the bushes. During our seance, everyone was in on the plan, except Jerry of course. "What was that?" Another person said, "Did you hear that?" We all said, "Something is in the bushes!" The only boy in our group was certainly not a macho one. He refused to investigate and save us from the monster in the bushes. I ended up going to get the damned hand and bringing it to the circle. Even though our plan bombed, it was the only real attention that hand ever received. I had finally concluded that function was extremely more valuable than cosmetics.

"The only way that we can live, is if we grow. The only way that we can grow is if we change."

~ C. JoyBell C.

A past life

Chapter 13

My Mechanical Journey

I was fitted with my first prosthesis when I was 8 months old. I couldn't crawl with one arm and didn't have the balance to learn to walk. The solution was for Robin-Aids Prosthetics in Vallejo, California to build my first manually operated prosthesis. It was supposedly the smallest one ever made at that time. It had a nylon harness that crossed behind my back and circled under my right arm to keep it secure on my body. The hook was rubber and had to be opened manually by my right hand to hold anything. I was told my story was in a medical journal in the late 50's, although I have never seen it.

I was sent to Shriner's Hospital for Crippled Children in San Francisco for physical therapy. Its name has since been changed to Shriners Children's Hospital. I could already pull tissues out of a box, open windows and doors of a playhouse and pretty much every other task they gave me by then. There was only one issue. My parents told the doctor I was beating up the furniture. The doctor said, "Well, spank her." That's how my discipline began. It's also how I was taught to never say "I can't". I was encouraged to keep trying until "I could". Don't get me wrong. I wasn't spanked to keep trying, but to teach right from wrong. The doctor's advice also taught my parents to never give up and to treat me like I wasn't any different than other children. I wasn't babied or coddled at all. This applied to every situation in my life.

All my prosthetics were quite similar over the years, although the first one was completely manual. I had to open the rubber coated hook with my right hand. My mother said she would offer me a cookie; I would open and take one cookie with my hook and hold my right hand out for another.

The rest of my prosthesis' were fitted by making a cast of my stump to make a plastic (eventually silicone) socket. The fiberglass or plastic body was built around the socket and a leather upper arm was attached to it. The leather sleeve had buckles that attached a nylon strap that was worn over my shoulder, across my back and under my right arm. It was called a harness and was probably as uncomfortable as ones used by horses. It was hot in the summertime, inconvenient because undressing was necessary to remove it, and eventually caused cysts under my arm from wear and pressure. To open the hook, I would flex my shoulders causing the harness to pull a cable attached to the hook. Rubber bands kept the hook closed when not in use and allowed it to close automatically.

I was finally willing and able to move up in technology and afforded a myoelectric prosthesis in 1995. My husband, John, worked for the Navy at Mare Island Naval Shipyard in Vallejo, California. He had exceptional health insurance and used this opportunity to propose marriage to me. "Wouldn't you like to get a new arm? Shouldn't we get married?" He was such a romantic!

My new prosthesis was a game changer (along with my new husband, of course). Although the base looked the same, including a functional hook, it was controlled by an electrode in the socket. By sensing muscle movement from my stump, the electrode signaled the hook to open. My current arm has two – one to open and one to close the hook. I'm finally able to hold a tomato to slice it without smashing it. I can finally wear dresses and blouses without having to worry about exposing an ugly harness over my shoulders. The prosthesis is held on by a pull-down method as it is tightened above both sides of my elbow. There is no more need for anything to hold it up by straps. This is how I'm able to easily remove it and throw it into a basket at the airport! It's the little things in life, isn't it? LOL

"If you can dream it, you can do it."

~ Walt Disney

Left – Danny Husband #1 & #2
Middle – Charles Husband #3
Right – John Husband #4

Chapter 14

Dream On

My dreams of the future have been the same for as long as I can remember. Like I have said earlier, I had hoped to be a wife, mother and happy homemaker. I wonder how much the old television series of my era influenced my ideas of what a good life looked like back then: Leave it to Beaver, Dick Van Dyke, I Love Lucy and of course, Bewitched. None of those mothers worked and looked happy in their perfect little lives. None of them had any limitations either. Surely, I could have that kind of life, and no one would expect any more of me. Or would they?

My first husband, Danny, had a different plan for me. He was in the Air Force when we got married the first time in 1977. I had no idea he wanted me to work until one day when he said, "Why don't you get a job?" It wasn't said out of anger or even as a joke. He seriously meant it. I thought I would challenge him and answered, "OK, if you do the laundry". To my shock and dismay, he agreed! I had no idea what to do, or more importantly, what I was capable of. One of my girlfriend's mothers told us she knew of a program funded by the California State Rehabilitation Department called the Comprehensive Employment and Training Act (CETA). CETA was a United States federal law signed by President Richard Nixon to train potential workers and provide them with jobs. This program was for low-income people and the long term unemployed. Its intent was to get more people to work by learning a marketable skill. A school opened just outside the main gate of Mare Island Naval Shipyard in Vallejo, California. The State bought me a Smith-Corona electric typewriter with an internationally known Dvorak keyboard for "handicapped" people. Mine was specifically for right-handed typists. Today the Dvorak keyboard is standard with Windows on all computers except Apple devices. I enrolled into Polly Priest Business College that participated in CETA and that was the beginning of my career as a clerk typist.

Polly Priest provided every course needed for a stenographer in their curriculum. This included: Business English, math, spelling, filing, Stenospeed (shorthand) and of course typing. I completed the program typing 55 words per minute with one hand and Stenospeed at 70 words per minute. I went to my first interview at Bank of America World Headquarters in San Francisco and got my first clerical position in the Employee Relations Department.

I will never forget my first day on the job. I lived in Fairfield, a small bedroom community 45 miles east of San Francisco. Traffic into the city was horrendous as well as stressful. So, I drove to Concord, by myself, to the Bay Area Rapid Transit (BART) train station. Dressed in a skirt and heels, carrying my specially made portable electric typewriter by the handle of its plastic case, I walked up to the machine and nervously put money in to purchase my roundtrip train ticket. I was 20 years old, by myself and lost. After figuring out what platform to depart from and what station to go to in the City, I got on the train, by myself, and sat down completely exhausted. Did I mention I was by myself?!

It was time to debark at the Civic Center Station on Market Street. It wasn't terrifying enough to leave the East Bay through an underwater tunnel to San Francisco, but now I was alone in a big city for the first time ever. I realized how young, lonely, scared and insecure I was when disembarking BART and looking at a bustling station with escalators leading into the sky. Everyone else walked with purpose toward their destinations. Not me. I stood there, terrified, out of my element, looking at all the possible exits and not knowing which one to choose. This was an important decision wearing high heels and carrying a heavy typewriter. In this situation one wants to choose the shortest path possible especially knowing the walk from the station to the Data Center building is two blocks...San Francisco blocks. I eventually chose an escalator and made my ascent. I stepped off the escalator, moved aside, set my typewriter down and looked both ways up and down Market Street. I saw homeless men sifting through garbage cans, people dressed in professional attire hurrying to work, and there I was - out of place, invisible and alone. I finally got enough nerve to ask someone directions. I knew it would be a long walk so it was very important to my feet to head in the right direction immediately. I made it in one piece, without incident, my feet throbbing like Fred Flintstone after stubbing his toe, and settled into a commuter's routine. I was eventually transferred to a local position with Bank of America after six months ending those 12-hour days caused by an exhausting commute.

Although my writing ability began with effortlessly drafting professional letters, it wasn't until I decided to go back to school for a degree in business that I discovered my true passion. I was already in my 40's and married for the fourth time. I enrolled in the local community college and chose English as the first class in what would have been a long haul working full-time, going straight to school after work and driving late at night back to the Sierra where we lived at the time. It was just something I couldn't imagine doing for many years - especially at my age. The English professor and his class changed my life forever, not only by becoming aware of my love for creative writing, but my grades proved I was actually pretty good at it. I was still going in the wrong direction, though.

The next class only led me further from realizing I wanted to be a writer. Community colleges in our area began offering online classes so I enrolled in a business administration class. This proved to be a real snore fest for me and all I could think about was getting through school hell as fast as possible. It never occurred to me that I was chasing a dream that wasn't mine at all.

A co-worker and friend at work began a degree program at the University of Phoenix. Her courses were on campus, but she told me the school also offered an online curriculum with an accelerated program. A Bachelor's Degree in a couple of years? Where do I sign up since I won't have one foot in the grave at graduation?

"Today is the future I created yesterday."

~ Louise Hay

Me and Kim

Chapter 15

The Last Hurrah

The first day of a new job is never easy for me. No matter how much confidence I have in my abilities, it is always the same. Most people are anxious or uneasy during an interview. Some are unable to answer questions as they allow nerves to take over. I am completely opposite. I go prepared with answers to possible scenarios. The Internet is full of information on interview questions, what purpose they serve, what answer employers are looking for, and how to conduct oneself. The primary reason I interview well, though, is because I am proud of my knowledge, experience, and skills. I know I can prove myself as a positive asset to a business with integrity. If that doesn't work, I throw in personality! I have been known to immediately break the ice to address the "elephant in the room", my arm.

This is the perfect opportunity to ease their minds, allow everyone to relax (mostly me), as well as inform them of my skills: Typing at 55 wpm, English major in college, ability to multi-task, and my background relative to the application. I am not someone looking for pity or asking someone to hire me to meet a quota for employing the disabled. I want to be taken seriously for being able to bring something worthy to a company; not what the company can do for me.

I was awarded my last position based on an excellent interview. One lady on the panel even warmed up by the end. She appeared to be the tough one, very serious and displaying no personality whatsoever. I know how to be professional, however, and decided to kill her with kindness and hope for the best by presenting myself with assurance. I was informed later by a phone call that I was hired based on merit and an excellent interview. And then it started...

There was a chill in the air during the first day on the job. Everyone was trying to be nice, but it appeared fake to me. Was it me? My insecurities? The old Laura was suddenly present: Am I good enough? Do they think I'm qualified with my obvious "handicap"? This initial training day was more uncomfortable than I had ever experienced. A little joke and small talk were met with serious, blank stares and looks exchanged by women who obviously preferred to remain strangers to me. I felt naked in front of a classroom.

The next day wasn't any better, although I showed up with a positive attitude. Surely, the feelings of the prior day were all in my head. Even if that wasn't the case, I was going to give it another shot. Pulling into the parking lot, I noticed a couple of women in their cars with their windows open. It was a sunny, beautiful, warm, and clear morning in the Sacramento community of Natomas. My assumption was they were enjoying the nice weather while waiting to go inside. Maybe they were surfing the web on their phones until the last minute or taking care of personal business before starting the workday. I opened the front door. Yay! My new, previously unused security badge worked! Not so fast Missy…the lady that watched me badge in and walk into my office met me inside. "Did you set off the alarm?" she asked. "No. I didn't hear anything," I replied. "Well, then someone didn't set the alarm last night!" she exclaimed dramatically. So many things were going on in my head, but I said nothing. The more I thought about it, the angrier I became.

I went into the supervisor's office and explained what happened including how I felt set up. She replied by taking the side of the other employee. She said, "I don't think she would do that on purpose". I said, "Then can you please explain to me why she did NOT tell me I couldn't go inside until someone cleared the alarm? She watched me go in and didn't bother to warn me. Her window was even open! I don't buy it." I walked out of the office and stormed back to my desk.

No one liked me. Some were better than others at disguising their true feelings, but the air was so thick I could cut it with a knife. I remember one day being in tears in my office. The door was open, and my lead shared our workspace. I exclaimed to her, "I HATE WORKING HERE! I HAVE NEVER BEEN TREATED LIKE THIS!" My co-workers knew exactly how I felt at that moment hearing my rant through the open door. I hated getting up in the morning knowing what would greet me after an hour long commute every day. Every Sunday included dread and depression. Hating Mondays took on a life of its own. Eventually I found out who took their cases to

Human Resources and Management, who lied to attempt getting what they wanted (me out), and exactly why I was being targeted.

My friend, Kim, was a high school friend of my husband, John. They even dated a few times shortly after high school. We originally met at a high school reunion, but only got to know each other at a party for old classmates she had at her house. We found we had a lot in common, liked or disliked the same things, shared "aha" moments quite frequently and became best friends fairly quickly. We began going places with our significant others like San Francisco Giants games, concerts, out to dinner, etc. We all still go to Cabo San Lucas every year where she has a timeshare affording us a relaxing week at her resort on the beach. We have remained good friends even though the job almost broke us.

Kim is the friend who said, "Are you tired of commuting? My department is hiring. Fill out the application online and interview for the position." So I did! The drama and motivation to ease me out began as soon as the other employees found out who my friend was. She was UPPER management. It didn't matter that two supervisors under her were mother and daughter. In fact, the daughter was who I talked to about the alarm incident! Additionally, there was another supervisor whose sister-in-law got hired. Let me just say many of my co-workers were women who were friends of employees if not relatives. This fact was kept from me by all of them but was eventually brought to light. It didn't matter that I was hired based on qualifications and my interview. The supervisors were not advised by Kim, or anyone for that matter, to hire me. They did so based on my own merit. You couldn't have told anyone else I worked with that, though.

AHA! So, it wasn't about my arm at all! The cold shoulders were about my being a friend of upper management. After all, I would surely be overcompensated, allowed to run amuck, receive preferential treatment, and be promoted before any of them! That was so far from the truth. In a way, it felt better that the reason was jealousy and fear rather than thinking my birth defect prevented me from doing a good job. That was two years I will never get back and I couldn't be any happier to be free of drama while enjoying retirement. Although it is unfortunate my last job was another negative learning experience, I guess I had a few more lessons to learn: 1) Never work for a friend – it's possible, but not easy, 2) Never think it's all about my arm – there are other obstacles besides the obvious, and 3) Not everyone is going to like me and it's their shit, not mine. I need to learn how to stop picking said pile of shit up! It's not mine.

"No matter where you go, there you are."

~ **Confucious**

My Other Family (Claudia's)

Left - Our Parents

Middle - Our siblings

Right – Home

Chapter 16

Learning to Run

Overcoming life's obstacles can be more challenging for one person and less for another. Certain obstacles also mold our lives into different shapes whether we consciously depend on what direction our lives take or not. Some choose resolution if awareness becomes a desired action. Some fear change, personal growth or a different way of life and instead remain locked in a less fulfilling existence. It IS familiar and cozy. The unknown is scary, but also prevents us from healing which was necessary for me to move on in a more positive light. For me, my struggles morphed into different forms: becoming an adult while still feeling like a child, becoming angry as a recipient of bullying or unwanted attention, and lacking self-love while expecting others to fill the empty hole in my core. It was easier for me to fill the emptiness with different men, drugs or running from pain in any way possible. Fortunately, a life filled with unhappiness, degradation and loneliness did not lead to death, incarceration or too much fear to resist taking action to repair the inner turmoil of my miserable self.

I grew up in a time where children could play hide-n-seek after the streetlights came on at dusk. We held pretend seances in the front yard after dark. No one locked their doors at night until a murderer named The Zodiac Killer came along. The neighborhood kids were like family. Still, I didn't feel the same as anyone and maybe a little inferior to all of them. No matter how close we got, or how many years we accumulated together I would always be the "different" one. I was the only one who felt that way of course.

My best friend, Claudia, had a sleep over one night. In those days all the neighborhood girls use to have slumber parties for birthdays and summer fun. Claudia and I were so close we were almost one person. We thought alike, had the same interests, and made great use of our imaginations, although she was much better at it than me. One year her dad set up the family tent in their backyard. We divided the inside into rooms of our make-believe home including bedrooms, a nursery for our dolls and a kitchen. She even made overstuffed chairs out of pillows and blankets for our pretend living room. We even dug a small trench around the outside and let water from a garden hose run through it so we would have a babbling creek around our playhouse. Obviously, water and price for usage wasn't a big deal back then!

One day, Claudia shared her photo album with me. Both of us compared our pictures often. We were always anxious to see what our individual cameras saw after the local drug store developed our film. And there it was. A picture of me at a sleepover, out like a light with my short, bare arm draped over my head and my mouth wide open. I always consciously kept my arm out of photos whether wearing a prosthesis or not. In fact, only very close friends saw me without my "arm" on. I hid it behind my back in public as a small child to ward off unwanted attention or feeling like a spectacle. You would think I would have been more embarrassed about my mouth being open!

I couldn't get that picture out of my mind, nor how it made me feel so exposed and vulnerable. Looking back now I realize this is where my insecurities were born, nourished and how they shaped my deeply embedded lack of self-worth, self-love, self...self...self-self-everything. I was always trying to hide from myself and the fact I could never change into a person with two hands. I would somehow have to get that picture because I hadn't accepted the fact that I would have to overcome my insecurity to be truly happy. I knew Claudia and her family were out of the house one day. Only her dog, Freckles was there, but he could be a problem. I walked up to the door and gently turned the doorknob. Sure enough, Freckles was right there showing his teeth and making the "I'm going to kill you" growl even though he had seen me a million times. I don't think it was my pleading or sweet talk, but he let me in without even offering a treat. This dog was very food driven but indulged me anyway. I should have thought this break-in through more. I scurried down the hallway to Claudia's bedroom with my heart pounding inside my chest. The last thing I wanted was to be caught. I grabbed the photo album with the picture from hell in it and found it quickly among the pages. I removed the photo from between the cardboard page and clear sticky plastic holding it in place. I hid it under the carpet in front of her closet. I guess

I didn't take it because it would be considered stealing, so I just hid it from her hoping she'd never find it. I ran back down the hall to the front door to find Claudia's brother getting out of his car in the driveway. What do I do? WHAT DO I DO? I hid crouched behind the door. You know...the kind with the French windows that I could also see through coming down the hall. He opened the door. I popped up like I was purposely trying to scare him! He asked me what I was doing. I answered, "Just looking for Claudia". He seemed to accept my answer, offered her whereabouts and I said, "Oh ok" and ran out the door!

This is how I have felt most of my life. Conscious of my arm, wanting to be inconspicuous, hiding it so no one would notice or want to talk about it, and this way of life weaved itself into my adulthood without my even being aware of it. I had no idea what a relief it would be to just accept it instead of trying to ignore it, and just move on. No one could have told me letting it go wouldn't kill me. Practicing and acting as if I was ok would eventually FEEL ok. Act as if and you shall be. Really.

Unfortunately, the equation of acceptance looked like this: Insecurity + Denial + No Self Love = DASH. The DASH equals almost 40 years and represented every possible way I could think of to fill the empty hole in my soul. The Dash also includes all the ways of running when different placebos and temporary fixes failed to work.

"The attempt to escape from pain is what creates more pain."

~ Gabor Mate

Left – our dark days

Middle – 1994 Narcotics Anonymous Convention

Right – Current SPCA volunteer

Chapter 17

Going to hell slowly in a hand basket

The first method of running was discovering the opposite sex. Why did turning to different men work for a while? Men became a powerful coping skill almost immediately after losing my virginity. My newly found self-confidence was born when I learned I had something the opposite sex wanted. Being attractive to men was a great feeling. It was euphoric, gave me some self-confidence and became somewhat of an addiction. I wanted to learn everything I could about how to please a man including how to dress nice without being provocative. I believe in order to be good at something you have to love it. Sex was no different in this case. I felt more powerful the more proficient I learned to be in bed. It just wasn't enough. Even though it taught me I was attractive to men and my arm didn't make me unique enough to live a celibate life, it only led to shame and lower self-worth.

I never saw what happened next coming. My addictions have all happened gradually. I smoked a joint for the first time at 16. It wasn't for me, although I continued smoking in certain social situations over the years occasionally. I tried Cocaine next and liked it, but it was too expensive for my liking. Alcohol wasn't something I drank on a regular basis either until much later.

I will never forget the first time I used methamphetamine. We called it "crank" back then. I watched one of my friends line the white powder up on the mirror with a razor blade. It was nothing new. That was how I saw cocaine prepared. Then came snorting the line up my nose through a shortened plastic straw. My feelings came in this order: "OH MY GOD THAT BURNS! This tastes nasty dripping down my throat – not at all like coke. I'm never doing THIS again." What followed almost instantly was a feeling of euphoria I would be chasing for many, many years. I wanted to feel like that for the rest of my life.

Staying up all night playing cards and dice with friends became our primary entertainment for years. We laughed, enjoyed competing and spending quality time with friends. We embraced the party lifestyle and I look back on it as a great period of my life. After all, if it wasn't so much fun, I never would have kept doing it. That is the truth. It was a blast. Until it wasn't.

I stopped using for three years when my daughter's father and I were caught red-handed. My daughter unexpectedly walked into our bedroom and spotted a line of crank on the dresser. It had just been left for me, but she made it into the room before I could get there. Michelle confronted us with her discovery and her dad responded, "We put it there to see what you were learning in the DARE (Drug Abuse Resistance Education) program at school". We envisioned losing our daughter to Child Protective Services (CPS) along with everything we had worked so hard for and decided to quit. Everything was removed from our house by the next day. We were done.

Fast forward to three years and two divorces later when I went on a date with John. He said, "Do you want to go to a party?" A disclaimer followed, "There might be something lined up there", he said. I answered, "Sure – I've said no for three years. I can say no tonight too". Sure enough, my drug of choice presented itself at the party. It didn't even have to be gift wrapped in a pretty package. I saw it on the mirror, took it up my nose and my addiction began again just that fast. Unfortunately, the end wasn't pretty at all.

The first time I quit using didn't end because something tragic happened, or extreme consequences forced us to make a good decision. We quit to avoid those circumstances. I wasn't so lucky the second time.

"Insanity is doing the same thing over and over again but expecting different results."

~ Albert Einstein

Our first real date

Chapter 18

Making the Same Mistakes

My drug of choice snuck up on me like a mountain lion stalking its prey, pouncing on it, and eventually taking it down. It was patient, slow and eventually successful. I had tried different types of weed, but that high was never really my thing. It made food taste better and made sex a LOT better. I could still live without it. Cocaine was great at first, although it was too expensive since one wanted another bump every 20 minutes. Again, nothing I couldn't live without. Besides, Danny didn't like spending that kind of money on anything. We found cheaper entertainment and that's when I found my ultimate drug of choice - even over men.

Methamphetamine gave me the feeling I had been chasing all my life. Euphoria is generally defined as a state of great happiness, but this was so much more than that to me. Finally, something worked to fill that empty hole. Not only did I feel I could I run the quarter mile, but I didn't need anything or anyone else. I was confident, very awake, not hungry, and so energetic I could clean our kitchen baseboards with a toothbrush - all while being happy. There wasn't enough time in a day to do everything I wanted: cleaning, rearranging Tupperware, plucking my eyebrows to the extreme and shaping a heart out of my pubic hair with tweezers. I could be up for three days on $20. Perfect! I can still go to work and stay up all weekend to get things done or play cards with my friends all night. My second brush with addiction, as well as my relationship, was entirely different.

I have been married to my husband for almost 30 years. Has it been easy? Hell no! Has it been the easiest out of the other three failed marriages? Yes, in some ways and absolutely not in others. It has definitely been the hardest in the sense that we keep working on it no matter what it takes. There are several very important reasons why I don't want to train a new one - I mean - why it works this time - probably all of which were never obvious to me:

John is the love of my life instead of just being before who comes next.

I met John in a local pub in late October of 1992. A mutual friend of ours was a part-time bartender and asked me to keep her company in the bar one night. Weeknights were mostly slow for her there. So, I agreed to go. I hadn't been there very long when a tall, dark-haired man with a black mustache walked in. He was dressed in clean blue jeans, new white tennis shoes with green accents and a light windbreaker-type jacket that matched the specific green color on his shoes. I remember thinking, "How did he ever match those greens? He must have a wife". Our friend, Sharon, introduced us immediately. There was no one else in the bar. The next thing I noticed was his eyes. Although they were behind thinly framed black glasses, I could still see the unique goldish-brown eyes with the longest dark eyelashes I had ever seen. I was instantly smitten. BUT I was married to Husband #3. I am ashamed to honestly admit a committed relationship never stopped me from jumping out of one relationship into another.

After our initial introduction at the local bar, John and I were obviously interested in each other. My usual conflicted feelings happened immediately. An angel on my left shoulder reminded me of my marital status.

She was saying, "I know you aren't happy. I know your husband has stopped paying attention and listening to you. I know things haven't turned out the way you had hoped or planned. It's wrong to begin a relationship without properly ending another." She, the angel, worked...for a minute.

One night, a few days after I met John, we were sitting next to each other at the bar. I looked up to see a pen sliding down the bar toward me. A small piece of paper had been placed in the pocket clip. I removed the note to find the sender's phone number. Without looking at the man who sent the message, I looked at John and asked, "Can you please take me to the Harvest Dance right now?" I don't remember if we had been talking about this annual event, or if we both knew this was the night, but John said, "sure" and we left immediately. The angel on my left shoulder was still talking and so far I was still listening. What could be wrong with two friends going to a public event together? Surely, we would be safe in public. We hadn't done anything questionable...yet. There wasn't anyone on my right shoulder egging me on either. After all, John was removing me from the proposition I left at the bar.

We drove out to the annual Harvest Dance at the Cordelia Fire Station. Established in 1918, the home of Cordelia Fire Protection District (CFPD) still provides Fire and EMS service to the communities of Green Valley, Rockville, Cordelia, and lower Suisun Valley to this day. All are rural surrounding areas of Fairfield, California, our hometown.

The dance, also called the Cordelia Stomp, was actually the Fireman's Ball sponsored by CFPD as a fundraiser. The "Stomp" was usually the first Saturday in November. This particular night was Saturday, November 7, 1992. It would be the very last harvest dance in Cordelia and the night of our very first kiss.

I really don't remember much of the dance for some reason. Band not very good? I don't recall, but we ended up at another bar named Billy Joe's that was connected to the local bowling alley. We had a drink inside and John asked, "You wanna go bowling?" Now, I love to bowl. My middle school P.E. teacher was Miss Pat Costello who won 25 professional bowling titles including seven major championships: Four titles in the PWBA Players Championship (1971, 1972, 1974 and 1976) and three victories at the U.S. Women's Open (1972, 1976 and 1980).

She took our class on field trips to Fairfield Bowl on several occasions to teach us the sport, but it didn't help my game at all!

I answered, "YES" to bowling that night. Not only do I suck at this game, but I also happen to love it. And how much trouble could I get into while holding a bowling ball?

John took my hand to lead me to the lanes through a narrow, slightly dim lit hallway connecting the bar to the bowling alley. As we entered the hallway, just outside of sight, he twirled me around like an old-fashioned dance move, pulled me to him, held me in his arms, and planted the most tender, romantic, and sexy kiss I've ever felt. And there he was...the guy on my right shoulder: "Go ahead. You'll be fine. You're married but worry about that later. Your marriage is ending anyway. So, who cares? Just go with it". The angel on my left shoulder shut her mouth, at least for a while. We actually did bowl that night in between kisses. I was the happiest I had been for a couple of years.

We began seeing each other exclusively after the bowling night. I moved out of my condo and marriage into my own apartment and filed for divorce after only a year of marriage to Husband #2/Marriage #3.

Everything was looking like my happily ever after until...the party we went to that woke up my addiction. The monster I managed to keep asleep for so long was now wide awake. I also learned John was using my drug of choice all along. I had no idea. He looked so normal to me – not like a "tweaker" at all.

And THAT was the beginning of the end for me. If you have always had more sense to refrain from using a mind-altering substance, I envy you. I found out I am an addict in the process. I had no idea how intense the effects of a drug like this could be. All I wanted was to feel that way forever. You see, but most of you probably don't see, this euphoric state is the best feeling ever. Until it's not. One never knows when that day may or may not come. Fortunately, for me, it did.

"Rock bottom became the solid foundation on which I rebuilt my life."

~ J.K. Rowling

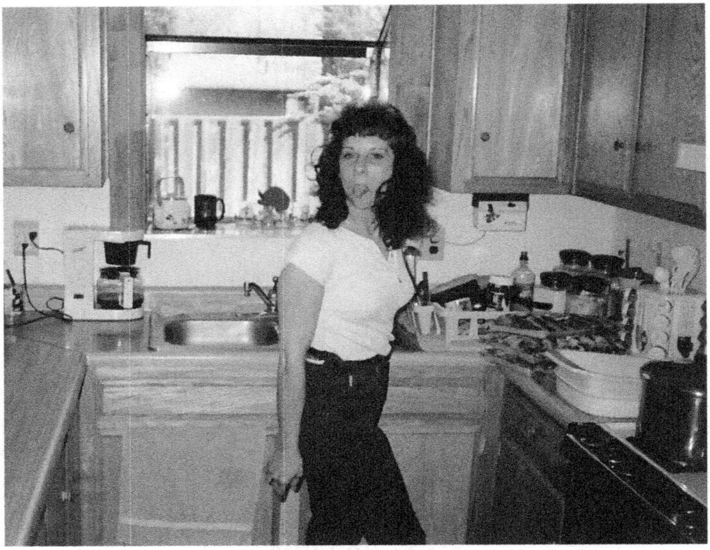

Chapter 19

The Last Snow Day

"In a dark time, the eye begins to see" – THEODORE ROETHKE

The day I used methamphetamine (crank) for the last time was January 30, 1994. Almost a year before john and I were married, the bag was empty and the inevitable melt-down, knock down, drag out arguing began. I have no recollection of how the fight began, or what was said during the entire screaming match. I believe it went something like this: "if you would stop bringing this shit home..."and John responded with something like, "it's not like you're not doing it too!" I knew without a doubt my daughter heard it upstairs. He outed me!!! I felt embarrassed and like the worst mother ever. I couldn't possibly stay there. Time to run as always!! The problem with my standard mode of operation was *I* was still ***there*** no matter where *I* went.

Withdrawal symptoms from crank are: depression, feelings of hopelessness and thoughts of suicide. For me, those symptoms always kept me looking for the next bag. Clearly, the drug had outlived the fun, euphoric stage and planned to remain in the ultimate survival stage. At this particular moment I felt the lowest ever. My secret was out and the one I loved most in the world knew it. The one I was supposed to guide, protect and set an example for. The worst feeling I've ever known was being a bad mother. I had failed my most important job – my most important reason for living at that time..

I ran out of the house in socks, no shoes and without a jacket. I left my 14-year-old daughter at home. I couldn't take her with me because of what I had to do. I was a terrible mother anyway. I didn't deserve another chance to screw it up even more.

I jumped into my car having no idea where I was going and sped off (ran away). I remember thinking it would be the last time I would have to run. Thinking. Thinking...but how? What would be the fastest, easiest way? I didn't have a gun. I had no pills that would end this thing immediately either.

I stopped at the local drugstore for some ambition. I grabbed a bottle of wine thinking it should be enough liquid courage. I wondered what the cashier thought of the distraught, crazy lady in socks who paid for these items and a package of razor blades.

I got back in the car and looked for a cheap motel. At least if I chickened out, I'd have a bed to sleep in. I checked into the room, grabbed a pad of paper, found a pen, opened the bottle of wine and wrote two suicide notes – one for my daughter, Michelle and one for John.

Some people think suicide is selfish when in fact it was quite the opposite in my own head. I felt irrational. My thoughts were trying to convince myself everyone would be better without me. I was doing them a favor. I felt hopeless, beyond sad, ashamed, unworthy of life or love, and extremely scared. I wanted to get on with my demise, but also wanted someone to talk me out of it. I felt like a bunch of different people in my head were all talking at the same time. "SHOULD I DO THIS? I WANT TO! I CAN'T GO BACK AND FACE ANYONE NOW! Or can I? If I do this,

I'll never have to feel this way again. I won't have to carry any more guilt. I won't be able to screw anyone else up."

I placed both notes on the nightstand and took a long swig of wine. I had to say goodbye. I had to hear their voices one more time. I picked up the motel phone and dialed home. John answered. I told him I loved him and wanted to say goodbye. I don't remember much more than that, but I asked to speak to Michelle next. I told her I loved her no matter what happened. She said OK and didn't give me any reason to change my mind. I'm sure she had her own feelings of abandonment and anger, but that's her story to tell.

John was able to find out where I was by dialing *69, a code used to call back the last number received. Motel 6 answered and gave him my location. The police were called as well. Meanwhile, I attempted to slit my rest with a razor blade teetering back and forth in my hook until my rescuers arrived. The police informed me suicide is illegal and took me to the emergency room to get my wrist addressed before taking me to a crisis center instead of jail.

We went to our family therapist the next morning. We had been taking Michelle to a psychiatrist for counseling, as well as to teach all of us effective communication. She saw my bandaged wrist and expressed her disappointment. She told us both to get into a 12-step program, go to 30 meetings in 30 days, get a sponsor and work the steps. She said, "then come back and we'll do some real work." We took her suggestions, Michelle finally came back home from running away, and our lives completely changed for the better.

I remain eternally grateful for this horrible experience. I believe everything happens for a reason and allows us to evolve into who we ultimately become. I have learned some extremely valuable lessons. Unfortunately, I mostly insisted on learning the hard way, but I'm glad I'm still here. It turns out I wasn't finished learning.

"Alcohol is a drug...Period."

~ Narcotics Anonymous, Page 18

6 months before clean AND sober

Chapter 20

Second Verse – Same as the First

I managed to put together a couple years clean, but decided alcohol wasn't a problem for me. I drank "successfully" for 25 years. It slowly began with a glass of wine at dinner. Then a day here and there, almost every day, and some days all day.

Drinking never became a big deal until my substance of choice became Vodka martinis. Wine, champagne, a screwdriver, Bloody Mary or my old go-to drink of Seagram's and Seven-up were fine. I was on a Cosmopolitan kick for a while too. Champagne, or sparkling wine, was also a drink of choice for years. I was the type who could open a bottle of wine, have a glass or two with dinner and put the cork back in the bottle. I should have never started drinking martinis. And let's be honest. My martini was straight vodka, shaken over ice, and served in a pretty class with olives. NO VERMOUTH either. Blech!

As soon as I turned this corner, normality and sensibility left my way of thinking, acting, and living. I became happy, relaxed, and confident with the first drink. I became combative, belligerent, and argumentative by the third martini. However, the first martini was all I needed to bring on aggressive conduct at the end of this run. I managed to convince myself and John that only vodka caused my bad behavior. So, I switched to Tequila. Shots.

Instead of having a cocktail while getting ready to go out to dinner or any social gathering, I was doing two, three or four tequila shots. It had become a reward after cleaning house or running errands. If it wasn't a shot or more of tequila before going to a Giants baseball game, or any social event, it wasn't a proper celebratory beginning.

The ending of this addictive behavior was almost exactly like the first one with drugs in that I never saw it coming, I believed everything was fine when it absolutely wasn't, and the final run took me down a long, dark, familiar road.

Depression, hopelessness, and the inability to "SAVE" my daughter was an excuse to drink more, numb more and as crazy as it sounds, it turned out becoming exactly what I was trying to convince her to stop doing. My husband was who I took it out on. We couldn't communicate if our lives depended on it. I believed he antagonized me when I was drinking just because I "could" drink and he couldn't. I was really running from reality just like I had always done. I was using the same method only with a different substance.

I crashed and burned Easter Sunday 2022. Finding myself in a familiar place of being sick and tired of being sick and tired, I washed down a bunch of Xanax with a couple shots of tequila and went to bed. I didn't want to die, although it had entered my mind like the time before. I just wanted to go to sleep for 15 hours to escape. The inability to help my daughter in her addiction, let go of everything I had no control over, and feeling like "Oh fuck it – I give up" sent me spiraling again 28 years after the first time. I will be forever grateful for this major meltdown because it made round two of recovery possible.

Being clean **and** sober this time has afforded many opportunities. Finishing this memoir is among them. More importantly, I have never felt better, healthier, and clearer in my mind. My husband and I have become a real team again. It seems like we were just pretending before. We actually communicate effectively on an adult level. We are finally on the same playing field.

In addition, I have been able to find my real interests again. Alcohol had become a priority. I had forgotten about all the other things that used to make me happy; i.e., my husband, healthy relationships, keeping an organized, clean home, feeling better about myself by helping others, and many more. I also found my love for music again.

"Where words fail, music speaks."

~ Hans Christian Andersen

My mother, Michelle and my organ

Chapter 21

Music is My Life

Music has been a major part of my life since I can remember. The earliest recollection is my father teaching me to do the twist to Chubby Checker's "Soda Cracker" and being influenced the most rhythmically by "The Twist." I can still picture myself moving my arms and waist in opposite directions, learning to feel the music, and smiling to "Come on baby...let's do the twist" in Mr. Checker's throaty voice. I was around 5 years old.

Not too long after that, The Beatles were on the Ed Sullivan show. My parents, along with over 70 million other people, tuned in that night on February 9, 1964. It would be The Beatles' first live performance in America. My father said, "Laura, look! It's The Beatles." I couldn't imagine why he would want me to look at insects on the TV. All I can remember of that debut was their long hair, the screeching female voices in the audience and a style of music I had never heard before. How was one supposed to dance to that? It was also the first time I noticed how a guitar was being played.

I found an acoustic guitar at my maternal grandmother's house one day. I had never seen it before and still don't know whose it was, but I was fascinated by it. I picked it up, started picking each string and wondered how it worked. My grandmother said, "You could learn to play that, Laura. All we have to do is have it restrung as a left-handed guitar." I had no idea why, but I was interested because of my love of music at such a young age. I don't remember ever seeing that guitar again. It disappeared just like a lot of things in my grandmother's house. Televisions among many other items grew legs and walked out of there on a regular basis.

We always had a music teacher in elementary school. Mrs. Ruff would bring in all kinds of instruments for us to play, but I always chose cymbals or something I was able to play with one hand. I can still remember feeling the disappointment and anxiety caused by my limitations. It seemed like such a sick joke that I couldn't make music when it was so important to me. I would be eleven years old before my introduction to music lessons.

Our next-door neighbor owned an organ and piano store. My father actually went to work for him as a sales manager. The owner originally sold my parents a small Baldwin organ with two stacked keyboards and a small pedal board. He eventually "gave us" a Baldwin theatre organ with two keyboards, sound pre-sets, an acoustic rhythm box and a full-sized pedal board to produce the low-pitched bass line of music. I believe my parents continued making payments on the small organ, but the theatre organ was in our house and considered a "gift" for my "progress". I took lessons and learned to play fairly well using my right hand to play chords on the lower keyboard and my hook to play melodies on the top row. My parents entered me in a talent show when I was 12 after I learned block chords (strengthening melodies by building the chord into the individual notes and playing them with one hand). I didn't win, but it was a good, although frightening and stressful experience, playing in front of an audience. Fear and insecurity were the primary reasons I lost interest. My parents asked me to play every time they had company. I also had to play at the piano store, in the front window, as the sound was piped through the entire outdoor mall. I felt like the star of a freak show as people came to the window to watch.

My parents eventually allowed me to quit lessons. I told them I was bored with the available sheet music and thought I was incapable of getting any better with my limitations. Playing chords with my right hand, pecking out melodies with my hook and playing with both feet on the pedal boards was about all I could ever do. Still the requests to play for family and guests never ceased. Same old shit – just a different day. SNORE!

To this day I love all kinds of music that began with the interest to appreciate all instruments and their separate roles in a song. I have always been enthralled by how each sound worked together to make harmonies, or even instruments battling against one another yet coming together to raise the hair up on my arms.

Each phase of my life is time stamped by assorted styles of music. It began with rock and roll from the 50's. Then came the 60's and pre-teens. This era brought jazz, pop, and folk music. Particularly interesting was the music that had a rebellious edge that protested the Vietnam War, the "free-love" movement and hippy generation.

My first concert was in 1969. I was eleven years old and had absolutely no idea how influential this event could have been for me. My girlfriend, also named Laura, asked me if I wanted to go. Her mother called my parents to get permission and off we went to Muir Beach near San Francisco in Marin County, California. I only remember a few things from that day: 1) the traffic was horrendous – like a bunch of mice trying to all go through a small hole in the wall at the exact same time, 2) there was music – very loud music and a LOT of people were dancing, smiling, waving their arms in the air and having what looked like the time of their lives, 3) many people were taking their clothes off. This is where my memory ends. Laura and I had never seen a penis before. We were simultaneously disgusted and amazed. We covered our eyes and looked through our fingers. We couldn't help ourselves from walking around to investigate our introduction to nudity. We saw a couple having sex behind a large boulder and decided we were probably going to be struck blind or go to hell for seeing this at our age. If my parents knew it was a nude beach, I never would have been there. Concert? What concert?

I saw Laura's mother at a local restaurant many years later. She was a server there and recognized me immediately when I ordered lunch one day. She asked me if I remembered going to a concert with her, her sister and her daughter, Laura. I said, "You mean the one where everyone was taking their clothes off?" She said, "YES! Do you remember who we saw?" I had to admit I had absolutely no idea. Regretfully, I must live with the fact my first concert was Janis Joplin and Jefferson Airplane AND I DON'T REMEMBER IT. AT. ALL. This will forever be the one thing in my life I would consider being hypnotized to remember. I wish I could say, "My first concert was Janis Joplin" without having to immediately follow it with "But I don't remember it"! So, my next live show remains the real first concert and has become the most important for many reasons.

"What made me pick up a guitar? It weighed a lot less than a piano."

~ Ronnie Montrose

Ronnie Montrose

Chapter 22

A Brush with Celebrity

I received a phone call one day from my girlfriend, Rhonda. She said, "You have to come over and hear this!" There was so much excitement in her voice that I couldn't resist dropping everything and walking to her house. She showed me the album cover of four shirtless men with "MONTROSE" written diagonally across their images in pink letters. I heard the most amazing sound coming from a guitar when the needle of the record player hit the vinyl. The slide guitar lick, played by Ronnie Montrose, simulated a motorcycle revving its motor. This girl was hooked (no pun intended) from that moment on.

March 12, 1976, marked the day I have to remember as my first concert. Montrose, featuring Ronnie Montrose (guitar), Bob James (Vocals), Denny Carmassi (Drums) and Alan Fitzgerald (bass) at Winterland in San Francisco would change my life forever. This would be one of many concerts in various incarnations including solo shows as well as his next band, Gamma. Sammy Hagar, former lead singer for Montrose, actually opened for Ronnie that night. Always a day late and a dollar short, as I had to wait over 20 years to see the original line up when Sammy added the original band members to the final set of his show in Reno, Nevada. This was the beginning of my appreciation for exceptional guitar work and way before my fandom became a cherished friendship with my idol. Ronnie gave me and the world more than he ever knew was possible.

He gave us a lot of gifts without realizing how important and meaningful they were. My first phone call from him was the second gift he gave me. I remember each detail as if it were yesterday. The receptionist at work called on my phone intercom and said, "Ronnie is on Line 1". I said, "thank you", but thought it was my cousin, Ronnie. I identified myself to the caller who said, "Uh yeah, Laura, this is Ronnie Montrose". I said, "No it's not". He said, "Yes, it is." I said, "No way"! Surely, someone in the office was playing a trick on me. Where was the hidden camera? Then he asked, "Would I shit you?" with a little giggle at the end. I knew it was him. I had heard his voice a few times at concerts. My girlfriend, Rhonda, once yelled, "ALRIGHT RONNIE" in the middle of a guitar solo at the Old Waldorf in San Francisco. He stopped playing and said, "Alright yourself" and picked up right where he left off. I could have knocked her over with a feather.

The purpose of the call was to thank me for responding to a question. I had sent a personal email to RonnieMontrose.com requesting show information. The website was fairly new; the EVENT section was empty. I had no idea if he was touring at all. He emailed me back with information for a show in Sacramento at The Roadhouse. Ronnie also wanted to know if I could recommend a quiet getaway in our area. He was living in El Dorado Hills – another connection we had because it was only 15 miles from my work. I put together an email with three places including photos and reviews. My work contact information was listed at the bottom because I sent his response from my office. So he called me to thank me and invite me to the show personally. That is how I met my friend, Ronnie.

My daughter and I showed up to The Roadhouse, a night club in Sacramento, California. Several bands were playing that night including members from Night Ranger and the Doobie Brothers. I remember seeing Ronnie running back and forth checking equipment before the show and thinking how much different he looked than the last time I saw him, as it had been many years since my last concert with him. We met on the patio outside the venue and chatted for a while. He graciously asked questions to get to know us and we immediately felt comfortable being in his presence. Ronnie was just that way...easy to get to know, humble and so unaware of just how special he was; not just to me, but to everyone who was fortunate enough to meet him.

Several phone calls and shows followed over a couple of years. A couple of them stand out in my memory. He called me one day especially to tell me he was putting me and John on a guest list. He was opening for Dave Mason at Harrah's in South Lake Tahoe. Ronnie said, "You have to come. Dave Mason is an incredible musician and I am honored to be playing on the same bill with him". It was the day after Ronnie's dad had passed away and he played his heart out anyway. I was never so glad I got to hug Ronnie on that day. My husband also gave him a big bear hug. Ronnie always loved John too.

We had a couple of conversations about my wayward daughter who was lost in addiction. He gave me some good advice over the phone. He said, "she'll come back to you" along with some personal information straight from his heart about his own family. It was also this same call when he asked, "So, what's up with your arm?" I started laughing because I hadn't even remembered my difference when we met. I was too busy being star-struck! I briefly answered his question that it was a birth defect, he accepted and that's the last time we discussed it. Again, that was Ronnie – to the point and unconditionally accepting of everyone.

We were invited to one of his weddings. Gift #3 – you see, this was when I knew I was a friend instead of just a fan. Now I was the "honored" one. The highlight of that evening was open mic at the reception. Everyone, no matter who they were, was invited to play. Ronnie had always said he never wanted to play Town without Pity live again; especially with no orchestra. BUT there it was. As soon as I heard the opening I stood there with my eyes on his guitar and tears rolling down my face. It had been the first time in 30 years I had heard it and would be the last.

I lost contact with Ronnie after that for several years. I saw some rumors on the Internet that he was ill. I gave it one more shot, a third attempt, and tried to contact him via email. He finally answered saying he survived prostate cancer, but not his marriage. I had mentioned that I feared I had done something to upset him and wondered if that was why he hadn't responded to the couple emails I had previously sent. His answer will haunt me for the rest of my life. He said, "Laura, if you think you did something to upset me, I have a phone number for a good therapist." Unfortunately, Ronnie Montrose took his own life March 3, 2012 due to clinical depression.

The very first gift Ronnie gave me was his talent. He was responsible for my changing genres from R & B (Stevie Wonder, Earth Wind & Fire, Tower of Power, etc.) to ROCK (Montrose, Peter Frampton, Steve Miller Band, etc.). I had always been more appreciative of drums and brass. I had no idea a guitar could be played like his. How did Ronnie do that?

One time he called me at work right after a co-worker and I had his song Voyager playing as loud as possible on our computer speakers. Both of us stopped typing/working and listened to his solo with our eyes closed. Afterwards, we both made this ahhhhh sound together. I told Ronnie he called at a perfect time – Brian and I were enjoying Voyager and making noises as if we were having orgasms. He said, "I'm gonna tell John!" It wasn't too long afterward that Sammy Hagar was at the Reno Hilton Amphitheater in Nevada singing with the original Montrose members in his last set. Brian came with us and at one point I looked over at him. We were both crying. Partly, because of how fortunate we felt to be there, but mostly because of the history we were witnessing. If only he knew how much we all loved him and appreciated his talent.

He has robbed us of ever seeing him in the flesh again, hearing his guitar live and just being in his presence, but not without giving all of us his precious gift. I am grateful I got to know him as well as experiencing first-hand what he had to offer the world. Thank you to Ronnie Montrose for everything he gave us. I will miss him forever. Especially since I will never be able to show him how he inspired me to finally pick up a guitar.

"Music is the shorthand of emotion."

~ Leo Tolstoy

Left – Richard, brother-in-law

Middle – Ronnie Kimball

Right – My guitar instructor Rick Lowe

Chapter 23

Make Your Own Kind of Music

I hadn't given much thought to my playing guitar over the years. My appreciation of the instrument was always about hearing accomplished musicians seamlessly play these mysterious strings. I had no concept of how chords or notes made music on a guitar even though I could still read music because of my organ lessons as a child.

A friend of mine introduced me to the video game "Guitar Hero" in my late forties. This was a rhythm-based Wii game using a controller plugged into an imitation guitar to simulate playing lead, bass or rhythm guitar. A player would match notes that scroll on-screen to colored fret buttons on the controller in time to the music in order to score points and keep the virtual audience excited. If one screws up enough, the game ends with the crowd booing the player's incompetence.

FINALLY! I could be a rock star! Or pretend to be one anyway. All it would take is some practice to get fairly proficient. I LOVED this game. Yet, it still lacked something. Maybe my being a musician, who could actually read music, caused me to want more. Maybe I felt I was cheating myself. Whatever the reason, my dream of playing an acoustic guitar still lived inside me. I still remembered the hopeful feeling while trying to play that old guitar at my grandmother's house.

My brother-in-law, Richard, could play guitar. He taught himself to play by ear. In fact, he said he just held it for a long time to get used to how it felt before he even attempted to play it. He knew I always wanted to play. So, when he saw an advertisement for a Keith Urban guitar he called to ask me if I would be interested and what color guitar I would like. The package included a beginner acoustic/electric guitar, amplifier, guitar case and lessons on DVD. Richard ordered a left-handed guitar for me even though I'm sure neither one of us were convinced I would ever be able to play it!

I popped the Lesson One DVD into the player and began learning how to tune my new toy. Keith Urban did a great job putting this together...for someone with a right-handed guitar. I found I needed more "hands on" LOL! I found it difficult to learn watching him, wondering if it sounded right and no one to tell me if I was using the correct fingers on the right strings. Even if it was right, I wasn't confident the guitar was even in tune, much less if I was playing it correctly.

Life happened after my feeble attempt to learn from Mr. Urban. So I put it away for a few years. Fortunately, I let guilt and shame take over and picked it up again. I couldn't forget about the gift my brother-in-law gave me; not just the guitar, but the confidence he had in me. I also had to shut my husband up. "Are you ever going to learn how to play that?" Oh, the sarcasm I heard over and over.

When I first got my guitar, I posted pictures of me holding it on Facebook. My dear friend, Ronnie Kimball, commented and offered to help me learn via FaceTime. This particular Ronnie is an old friend who used to play bass in a local band, LaserBoy. I love Ronnie musicians! Anyhoo – LaserBoy was a well-known band by locals and had lots of groupies – me included. The group included Ronnie Kimball (bass), Rick Lowe (lead guitar), Jeff Curtis (guitar), Chris Holmes (keyboards) and Paul Ojeda (drums). They recorded a video "One More Shot" and even got a spot on the night-time series Falcon Crest. These were two really big events for us local groupies!

I never took Ronnie up on his offer to teach me guitar by video call, but I did take a suggestion by him later. He recommended Rick Lowe, his previous band mate and friend, as an excellent guitar teacher. He said, "Rick is a great teacher. He's the one who taught me how to teach". Sounded good to me! A recommendation by someone I totally respect and love was much better than being a stressed out, nervous, self-conscious wreck in front of someone I admire deeply.

I called and made an appointment for my first lesson with Rick. I have followed a few bands he has played in after LaserBoy. I am very familiar with his guitar work and have admired him from afar for a very long time. He still plays in an R&B/funk band, Time Bandits and a country rock group called Whiskey and Honey. We had seen these bands numerous times before I began playing guitar, but I had never really met Rick until my first lesson.

I had to dress for the occasion by representing my friend, mentor and who originally inspired me to play the instrument. I chose a Montrose t-shirt picked out especially for me by Ronnie's wife, Leighsa, at the last Ronnie Montrose concert I attended. I packed up my guitar, grabbed my makeshift prosthesis and headed to Rick's studio. I believed my regular prosthesis with the hook was too long to reach the strings properly, so I had a rubber glove (typically used for casting) fitted to my arm. My husband attached a guitar pick to the end of it and it seemed to reach better as well as protect my instrument from being scratched by my regular prosthesis.

Rick was immediately welcoming and warm. I wanted to feel comfortable but was a bit nervous in front of someone whose talent I admired so much. We sat down in the studio to get acquainted. I proceeded to change out prosthetics, explain my limitations and show him my alternative solution to fingers holding a pick. He said, "Well, you know you're not going to be picking any time soon, right?!" We both laughed and got to work! Not only is Rick a good teacher, but he knows how to put someone at ease by breaking the ice!

Just like everything else, eventually I found a better solution than the rubber glove. I had forgotten my hook also has a "wrist" that moves toward and away from my body by the push of a button. It can be turned and locked into several different positions which allows me to place a pick in the hook and connect with the strings in the right place. One day I asked Rick to wait a second while I got my hook into position. I said, "Hold on" before we got started. He said, "What? You got a cramp?!" Just when I thought I had heard them all...! We laughed and laughed! I love his sense of humor. We have developed an incredibly special relationship. Not only do I have the utmost respect and love for him, but I am totally enamored with him. How brave of him to take me on as a student. What began as a challenge for both of us has now become a successful partnership and sense of pride for teacher and student. I can see it in both of us. I'm so grateful he gave me the gift of learning how to follow one of my dreams.

"Music is the fastest motivator in the world."

~ Amit Kalantri

Glen Burtnik

Chapter 24

Styx and Stones

The Story of the Drumstick

It was a winter's day in 1999 when I asked my husband, John, "What do you want to do for New Year's Eve?" Our typical New Year's Eves were usually spent safely at home. Besides, our daughter's birthday begins at the stroke of midnight every year as she was the first baby born in upper Solano County in 1980. I wanted to do something to celebrate this year and was surprised when John said, "I've always wanted to see Styx. Why don't you see if they're playing somewhere?" I immediately got on the Internet before he changed his mind and found they were playing at a casino in Reno, Nevada on New Year's Eve. I booked two tickets for the sixth row.

This also happened to be the year after the Y2K scare. I'm sure most people remember the end of 1999 as a ridiculous, fear-based rumor based on the assumption computers would be confused mistaking 2000 with the year 1900. Instead of buying into mass hysteria and trying to grab the last few bottles of water off the shelves and extra camping supplies, I was buying concert tickets!

There were 2 couples in the 5th row right in front of us that were bombed out of their gourds. They missed most of the concert. In fact, three of them left and the one remaining lady had her head in her own lap for the last part of the show. At the end of every show the Boyz, as the fans say, all come out and start throwing picks, monogrammed towels, beach balls with Styx on them, etc. Todd (my favorite drummer of all time) threw a drumstick into the crowd and hit the lady, right in front of me, on the head. She lifted her head up like "what was that?" I would have lunged for it, but my short dress and heels wouldn't cooperate. Like I said, we THOROUGHLY enjoyed the show, and a souvenir would've been great – the drum sticks are stamped with his name on them. I did want to grab the thing right out of her hand as she picked it up off the floor. Add insult to injury that she turned around to show me. SHE DIDN'T EVEN WATCH THE SHOW! Dumb broad (tee hee).

We attended around eight or nine shows after the drumstick debacle. We never sat down after that first show. It became mandatory to always be up front. I have guitar picks from everyone in the band. Some have been handed to me by the band member himself. Once Tommy Shaw bent over and tried to give me one and someone intercepted it. So, he got out another one – same thing happened. He finally grabbed my hand, opened it, put the pick in it and closed my fingers around it. It was pretty funny. He also leaned down at one show and put his guitar in front of me and told me to strum. I guess I can say I have played Tommy Shaw's guitar (ha ha). The original bass player, Chuck Panozzo, shows up at certain shows. He still plays with the band occasionally after giving up his full-time status after contracting HIV. It's always a pleasure and honor to see him. He happens to be a very NICE GUY too. Anyway, he threw a towel out and John caught it. The point is...I had acquired quite a collection from Styx. I had something from each of them except for a drumstick.

Eventually, three couples (all good friends) and us went to Konocti, a spa, resort and concert venue in Clear Lake, California to see them. Again. Desperate for a drumstick, I asked a very creative friend at work how to be recognized and successful. Especially, since I had spent most of my life being noticed for a completely different reason. My friend, Missy said, "Get a t-shirt and put I'd give my right arm for a Todd Styk" on it. She even made it for me! All of us went to the café at Konocti for lunch before the show. Glen Burtnik (bass player) was in there. I didn't want to bother him, but my friend Heath's daughter asked him to come over and get a picture with me. I could have crawled under the table and died of embarrassment. Heath took the picture of Glen and me. I said, "did ya get the t-shirt in it"? Glen stood back to see what I meant, read it and CRACKED UP! At the end of the show – we were at the front table of course - he motioned to me to stay there, ran back and got Todd from behind the drums, and brought him to me. We were all cracking up. AND that's how I finally got a drumstick!

"Life is like a camera. Focus on what's important. Capture the good times. And if things don't work out, just take another shot."

~ Ziad K. Abdelnour

Nonnie and grandbabies
Curtis John (CJ) and LauraSue

Chapter 25

~ THE END ~

There are many words meaning the end: Finish, conclude, terminate, draw to a close, stop, cease and reach a finale. Let's wrap this up!

Niccolò Machiavelli never said, "The ends justify the means". It is interesting that this well-known quote has been rephrased over the years. He actually said, "For although the act condemns the doer, the end may justify him" in The Prince. He said in Chapter XVIII , "Everyone sees what you appear to be, few really know what you are." These two statements are relevant to my story for two reasons: 1) Personally, I don't want you to think this memoir's purpose is to justify or rationalize my poor choices or behaviors. It is none of my business what you think of me. Your opinions and feelings are valid. They are yours just as mine belong to me. No one is wrong. 2) My memories may be different than someone else, but they are my reality and shared to the best of my ability. I have opened myself up to more judgment. I have had to accept that.

All my life I have felt misunderstood. It's really no one else's fault! I can't help the fact that everything I feel or think is plastered across my forehead. Unfortunately, most people assume to know how I feel. My "look" can be scary when I absolutely do not want it to be. I don't try to look like I want to kill someone just to convey my anger. I'd much rather use a healthier, calm way to express feelings, however, it's out of my control despite awareness.

People who know me best understand I act differently than usual when I'm hungry. A friend even gave it a name – "The Laura Syndrome". We went out to dinner with friends the last time my poor behavior presented itself. One couple was running late. No one was sure how late. They were "on their way", but were they ten miles away, a block from the restaurant, or even in the car yet? Everyone agreed to give them ten more minutes before ordering without them. This may sound reasonable to you, or at least not a big deal. Here's how I felt: "OMG

– I'm absolutely starving! I really wish we could at least get our salads, but we can't even order yet. It would be great to know exactly how long we'll be waiting to order." Here is what my forehead said, "ARE YOU KIDDING ME? I DON'T WANNA WAIT! I NEED FOOD NOW!"

The brief look from the person receiving my silent, misinterpreted reaction was all I needed to remind me how loud my forehead can get. She mentioned later she had to look away fast. Fortunately, it gave me the opportunity to sincerely apologize. I felt terrible.

This was just one example of how I have been judged, misunderstood, and misread over the years. Not just because of my arm, but my personality – over-sensitive, emotional, temperamental, and over-everything! LOL!

I felt it fitting and appropriate to end my story the same way it began. Who I think I am and how I wish others would remember me as a person. Am I perfect? Of course not. Am I terminally unique? Nope! Do I blame anyone else for my life? Absolutely not. We are all responsible for our own decisions and choices. No one is exempt from mistakes. We all, however, can choose to learn, change, and know there are rewards as well as consequences.

What has happened for me is a sense of gratitude. I wrote myself a letter to see what that looks like:

"*Dear Laura,*

I am thankful you finally got your head out of your ass. I am thankful for your new life, better communication skills, and a loving relationship with your husband. I am thankful you can be present for your granddaughter when her mother cannot be. I am mostly thankful your life looks and feels so much different now. I am thankful you're out of the fog.

I am proud of you for doing what is hard instead of remaining in the darkness even though it was a comfortable, familiar, and cozy way of life. Congratulations for working on yourself. Because of your courage you get to be present for the ones you love the most. Most importantly, thank you for learning how to love yourself. It has obviously been the only way possible to love anyone else completely.

Love you, for real

Laura"

Thank you, the reader, for letting me share my story. It really doesn't matter what you think of me. I just hope it may be helpful to at least one person out there who has struggled with being different and maybe failed a few times before getting it right. I wish nothing but the best for you all! Anything is possible if you follow your dreams and your heart. Empathy can be your guide too. It sure helped me!

Acknowledgments

Many heartfelt thanks to:

Claudia Grindle Montee. This book could not have been written without you. My life may have been very different without your love, support and hope you still give me in this sixth decade of our friendship.

Those who inspired me to follow my dreams:

- My fifth-grade teacher, Miss Lee Munoz, who taught me to love writing essays and detailed reports. This really all began with her.

- Jeff Goins, an author who said, "You are a writer (so start acting like one)". Without the 500 words per day challenge, I would have never known writing a memoir was possible.

- Leighsa Montrose, my friend first and intention

coach second. Thank you for your support and love. You are the reason my goals are attainable.

- My Brother-in-law, Richard, for not only buying me a guitar, but also having the faith I could actually learn to play it.

- All of my guitar GODS! To Ronnie Montrose for my love of the instrument and the friendship I will never forget. Ronnie Kimball for your love, support and recommendation of the perfect teacher for me. And Rick Lowe, the best, most patient, and talented guitar teacher I could ever have!

Ryan Mulford, who brilliantly designed my book inside and out. Thank you for your professionalism, patience, talent, and expertise. You have made me look so good!

My granddaughter, LauraSue Beverly Vaughan who teaches me every day how to be the best I can be. I am most grateful for the opportunity to pay it forward to her mother.

And last, but certainly not least, my husband John. Thank you for doing the dishes, making sure I ate, doing the laundry in the rain, and all the little, unspoken ways you supported me through this process. I appreciate your unconditional love and standing by me despite your awareness of every unflattering, explicit detail of my life.

About the Author

Laura Kendall is a new and upcoming author who recently discovered her birth defect was caused by the drug, thalidomide. After years of believing she was unique because of an "unknown morning sickness medication" taken by her mother, she now plans to bring awareness and knowledge to others by writing her stories. She has found a new passion to share, as well as being part of a comradery with other survivors of the thalidomide tragedy within the United States of America. Kendall uses her life experience to establish herself as an author worth reading, but most of all, someone who can understand the struggles of being different in a place where some strive to be accepted for who they are.

    She prides herself as an English major in business college, trade school, and the University of Phoenix

Bachelor of Science program. She worked for over 40 years as a clerical typist, accounting assistant, and even owned a typing service back in the day providing reports, term papers and resumes to her clients.

Laura spends her free time traveling, enjoying music/concerts, volunteering at SPCA of Solano County (a local non-profit animal shelter), and being a happy homemaker, wife, and grandmother. She is recently retired and living on the California Delta with her husband, John.

You can follow Laura on her website at laurakendallwriter.com, Facebook, Instagram and Twitter.

Made in the USA
Las Vegas, NV
28 December 2022